M

"Kristal's st
struggled w
heroine's jou
yearned. Th
triumphs."-
Pandemics,

"After thirt
to write a de
and class."-
New Midlife

"Kristal Bre
tale of trium
despite child
fully and ur
you."— KE\
in Photogra

the
girl
in the
yellow
poncho

Kristal Brent Zook

the girl in the yellow poncho

A MEMOIR

Duke University Press   *Durham and London*   2023

Printed in the United States of America on acid-free paper ∞
Project Editor: Lisa Lawley
Designed by Courtney Leigh Richardson
Typeset in Bell and Untitled by Westchester Publishing Services

Library of Congress Cataloging-in-Publication Data
Names: Zook, Kristal Brent, author.
Title: The girl in the yellow poncho : a memoir / Kristal
Brent Zook.
Description: Durham : Duke University Press, 2023.
Identifiers: LCCN 2022044181 (print)
LCCN 2022044182 (ebook)
ISBN 9781478017196 (hardcover)
ISBN 9781478024477 (ebook)
Subjects: LCSH: Zook, Kristal Brent. | Racially mixed women—
United States—Biography. | Racially mixed people—United
States—Biography. | Single-parent families—United States. |
African American extended families. | BISAC: BIOGRAPHY
& AUTOBIOGRAPHY / Cultural, Ethnic & Regional / African
American & Black | SOCIAL SCIENCE / Women's Studies |
LCGFT: Autobiographies.
Classification: LCC E184.A1 Z67 2023 (print) | LCC E184.A1
(ebook) | DDC 305.8/050092 [B]—dc23/eng/20221221
LC record available at https://lccn.loc.gov/2022044181
LC ebook record available at https://lccn.loc.gov/2022044182

Cover art: Cousin Lisa and the author, wearing her favorite
yellow poncho, circa 1973. Courtesy of the author.

An earlier version of chapter 13 appeared in the NewYorker.com
as "How Black Lives Matter Came to the Academy" (January 30,
2021); chapter 17 appeared, in a different form, as "Love Down
Under" in *Essence* (July 2002) and was reprinted in Taigi Smith,
ed., *Sometimes Rhythm, Sometimes Blues: Young African
Americans on Love, Relationships, Sex, and the Search for
Mr. Right* (Emeryville, CA: Seal Press, 2003).

contents

Gallery appears after page 110.

preface

There were interviews. Always interviews. Pen and notebook in hand, I rushed here and there, to appointments with television and film directors, producers, actors, athletes, and musical artists. As an entertainment and cultural reporter, I wrote features about Magic Johnson, Jamie Foxx, Jada Pinkett Smith, Keenen Ivory Wayans, Jill Scott, and Lil' Kim, to name just a few. Later, as I expanded into social justice reporting, there were politicians, activists, entrepreneurs, and all manner of change makers. I sat close as they laid out their speeches and plans, hoping that my words would also somehow contribute to the task of lifting as we climbed.

I saw myself as a race woman, in the old-fashioned Ida B. Wells sense of the word; a journalist who dug deep to lay bare injustices and hold a mirror to our collective trauma and triumph. I was down for the cause, despite what some may have seen when they looked at me. I knew that my nearly white appearance put me at the periphery of this landscape, and yet I claimed it as my own. Raised by my African American mother and grandmother, where else was I going to go? I was light-skinned, but for me, there was no question of being anything but Black. Still, for many years, I held on to a secret shame and deep insecurities.

My white father had abandoned my mother before I was born, sending a message that locked itself into my psyche. I was unworthy of a man's love. Unworthy of white protection. Unworthy of the picturesque (and always white) family life I saw on television. To add to my humiliation, a father figure next door violated my innocence as a child, confirming that I did not belong to the tribe of girls who were to be cherished. I wrestled with these demons of sexual assault, trauma, abandonment, and racial shame for the first four decades of my life. And when I say wrestled, I mean literally, knock down to the ground, kicking and punching, wrestled. I journeyed across oceans. I prayed. I counseled. Time and again, I beat back the temptation to sink into a long history of generational drug and alcohol addiction that was entrenched on both the white and Black sides of my family tree. I would be whole, I decided, even if I had to grab the devil of my past by the throat and wrench the air from his lungs in a gladiatorial do-or-die fight to the death. I did that. I took him on.

And I won.

Today, my lost father is found, and amazingly present. So, too, is my mother, an unexpected piece of my happy-ending puzzle. Somehow, against all odds, I've managed to create the family of my dreams, with a husband I adore, a lovely stepdaughter, and my sunshine, our six-year-old daughter. I could not have done that without faith, an open heart, and a determination to heal.

My husband and stepdaughter are from Spain, while my daughter is biracial, of African American and Southeast Asian heritage. Our household is undeniably multiracial, part of the rapidly expanding population that has only recently begun to explode into our collective national awareness.

So where does that leave me, the journalist who has written about blackness and race all her life? Who am I now, if not the reporter documenting the suffering and strength of Black women? My answer is this book. In it, I take a journey back to a time when I recognized the power of others to move mountains but couldn't quite see the brightness of my own star. This story is my testament to the power of forgiveness and settling into one's own authentic identity. In short, it's my rediscovery of a little girl who once stood tall and joyful in her favorite yellow poncho.

acknowledgments

For a long time, I thought this was going to be a book about finding and making peace with my father. Even before reading these pages, he supported the idea of this book without question. For his openness and willingness to be put on display, I am deeply grateful. In the end, however, this was also a story that belonged to my mother. At its core, it is a journey about intergenerational healing among the daughters, mothers, and grandmothers in our family. For helping me to find my way through this morass, I thank my mother for her grace and generosity throughout the often difficult process. Thank you to my grandmother, who has watched over the entire process, I'm sure, in spirit. My cousin Lisa is truly one of the most selfless people I know, always unflinchingly embracing my own goals and dreams as her own. When she was moved to tears by something in the book, I knew that my words were correct. Like all the women in our family, she is a true survivor.

My daughter, Olivia, has been my inspiration from the inception of this book. The brightness of her spirit guides my path in every way. I hope that she may one day take comfort from the love of family expressed in these pages and the love that envelops and surrounds her at all times.

Last, but certainly not least, I thank my husband, Alfonso, who perpetually reminds me that it is both my right and my duty to fly. He has expanded my soul in ways that I cannot fully express. Not only has he generously supported this telling of our family story, but he also deserves much of the credit for making our family possible.

It is one thing for an author to mine the depths of the soul to write a memoir. It is quite another to help a loved one do so. I thank my entire family for allowing me this honor. Just as these words have contributed to my own healing, may they also contribute to theirs.

Thank you to Gisela Fosado, Alejandra Mejía, Lisa Lawley, Courtney Leigh Richardson, Laura Sell, and the entire team at Duke University Press. It has been a pleasure working with all of you. Laura Nolan at Aevitas Creative Management, you are much appreciated. I am deeply grateful for the sabbatical time provided by my colleagues at Hofstra University in New York. It has been a long journey. Thank you also to Malaika Adero and Jill Petty for seeing the value in these pages long before they took their final shape and form.

the girl in the yellow poncho

kansas avenue

"California law requires rentals to be free of rodent and pest infestations," Mom said through a clenched jaw and festering indignation. "We put all that in the letter." After our landlord refused to exterminate our apartment, which was crawling with roaches, Mom had consulted with Legal Aid and discovered that she could pay for a fumigation service herself, deducting the cost from that month's rent. She was resourceful in that way. Smart. But now, her anger draped itself into the corners of our little secondhand Toyota Corolla, which she had scrimped and saved to buy. What a relief to ride in a car, I thought, staring out the window. No more trudging back and forth on the stinky bus.

Mom took a drag of her Virginia Slims cigarette, filling the car with smoke. From the passenger seat, my grandmother's face was steely. She sucked her teeth, considering the situation, and finally replied, "That man ain't shit." Dra, as we liked to call her, was only four foot eleven, but for me, and I suspect for my cousin Lisa, too, who rode beside me in the back seat, Dra was the most powerful force in our world. Anybody who risked her wrath, well, that was risking quite a lot.

Mom and Dra often had conversations like this one: bitter exchanges about no-good, two-bit male landlords or bosses. While most of what they said went over my head, the gist of their worldview was as clear as Mom's Helen Reddy soundtrack. We were Black. We were women. We worked hard. We struggled. Fighting back and being angry was the story of our lives, it seemed to me. Men, when they managed to stick around, only increased our heartaches. We might have enjoyed watching *Shaft* and *Super Fly* on-screen—cool cats who exploded into movie theaters in the early 1970s. But such men didn't exist in real life. Not in our world.

I didn't know it then, but Mom and Dra were laying a serious foundation for us girls, outlining the contours of a belief system I would take to heart so completely for the first few decades of my life that it never occurred to me how fundamental it was to my being. Or how detrimental. They taught us, both in words and actions, one all-encompassing lesson: Black women survive. Push past the fear, the sadness, the regret, and don't count on anyone but yourself. Just keep stepping. Most importantly, never take the time to acknowledge old hurts and vulnerabilities. Leave those where they are, raw and unhealed beneath seemingly impenetrable surfaces.

We were on our way home from Dolores's church, as they called it, near Pico and Vermont in downtown Los Angeles. Dolores was a Latina family friend who may or may not have been an actual member of the clergy but who shared the same spiritual beliefs as Mom and Dra. Her "church" was more of a storefront shop with a podium and several rows of folding chairs for services. Dra liked to stock up on her talismans there, purchasing green candles for money, white ones for protection, and black to ward off evil. They were thick and came in glass jars, allowing them to burn for days on end. Dra kept long rows of them alight across the entire length of her bathtub. This seemed perfectly normal to me as a child. Didn't everyone fill their tubs with burning candles?

We called it Dolores's church, even though she had a husband somewhere in the background. Maybe we discounted him because he was up to no good. "He don't want the mestiza no more," Dolores later confided to Mom when her husband left her for a whiter Latina. Of course, we all sympathized. In that much, Latina culture was the same as our own. We all understood perfectly well the power of light skin.

The demons were aggressive at Dolores's church. Sometimes they had to be physically chased from bodies. Once, when a demon burst forth from an adult man, the entire congregation leaped to its feet. "Get the kids out! Don't let him get inside the children!"

On other Sundays, we attended church services at the home of Madame Eula, an ordained minister whose congregation met in her South Los Angeles living room. Or maybe that was Reverend Richards. In any case, there were several Black women preachers we trusted. It seemed perfectly normal to us that they might pepper their biblical proclamations with prophecy. Why wouldn't they? No one in our family doubted the power of divination. Mom and Dra depended on psychics such as Madame Eula to guide our family's comings and goings and to help prepare us for future events.

A more traditional option was Calvary Baptist Church on Twentieth Street, where parishioners fell out into the floor with the Holy Ghost. On those Sundays, Dra loaded us girls onto the bus for a full morning of Bible classes, sermons, and socializing with the tall-hatted women who gathered there. But no matter where we went, the best part about Sundays was coming home. I longed for the moment when I could finally kick off my patent leather shoes and watch the *Flintstones* while Dra boiled hot dogs for our lunch.

I glanced at Lisa in the seat next to me. She was more like a sister than a cousin, really, since we'd lived together our whole lives. She happened to be biracial too: her mother was white and her father (Mom's brother, my uncle Mervin) was Black. Unlike me, however, Lisa had smooth black ringlets and olive-colored skin. I was more yellow-toned, with a frizzy, blondish-brown mane. Despite our different features, people assumed we were sisters. Some even asked if we were twins, perhaps because of our matching green eyes. Talk about color-blind. Our color apparently made them blind to everything else.

It's hard to imagine now, but in the mid-1960s, children of more than one race were still seen as strange. Until 1967, interracial marriage was still illegal in sixteen states. Our very existence warranted curious stares and rude pointing on a daily basis. Once, Lisa's father—a brown-skinned Black man—took her for a haircut at the Santa Monica mall. A couple of police officers pulled him aside, detaining him for questioning. *What was a Black man doing with this little white baby?* they wanted to know. Those were the times we lived in.

Mom was never quite sure how to describe us to strangers who often asked what we "were." She and Dra told them we were "half-white" or "mixed," if they really needed to know. And they really seemed to need to know.

Mom steered the Corolla onto Cloverfield Avenue, a few blocks from our apartment. Dra, who never had a driver's license, was a classic back-seat driver, comically slamming her foot into the floor mat whenever she suspected Mom should slow down.

At a red light, the car stalled.

"Shit." Mom turned the key in the ignition.

"Not again," Lisa mumbled.

"What's wrong with it?" Dra asked.

"The same thing that's always wrong with it." Mom said this as though the car breaking down was somehow Dra's fault. In reality, it was a piece of junk that had never worked. My poor mom had been sold a lemon with a hopelessly corroded engine. No matter how many paychecks she poured into repairs, it never stopped breaking down.

A couple of guys offered to push us to the side of the road. From there, we didn't have far to walk. Gathering purses, groceries, and, of course, bags of heavy candles, we trudged the rest of the way on foot.

When I think about the subtle and not-so-subtle ways in which my mother and grandmother passed on lessons of strength and fortitude, I'm reminded of three memories in particular: boxing, bleeding, and pooping.

Professional wrestling and boxing matches were our Friday night ritual. Lisa and I curled up in the back bedroom, munching snacks. Dra was propped up a few feet away, in her own twin bed, popping open a Coors. Between us was a small black-and-white television on a rolling cart.

"Get 'em, Thunderbird! Knock his head off!" we yelled at the television. Mom stayed in her room during these bouts, never quite acquiring a taste for knockouts.

"Hit 'em harder, you dummy! Break his arm!"

And on we went into the night. Our ritual served as more than entertainment. It was also a teaching moment.

So was the Saturday morning that Dra yelled at me for nursing a bleeding finger. Squeamish to a fault, I was the kind of child who fainted at the mere sight of blood, passed out cold on the floor of my pediatrician's office. But Dra wasn't having it. There was laundry to do, and I was supposed to be helping her and Lisa sort clothes. "Ain't nobody got time to worry about that finger!" she barked. I had expected sympathy, but her expression was one I'd never seen before and wasn't quite sure I recognized. Dra was actually . . . disgusted? By what, I'm still not sure, but I suspect it was a kind of frailty, or weakness, that made her most uncomfortable.

Then there was the problem of my poop. I was often constipated as a child, spending long stretches on the toilet. During these episodes, I would moan or cry out in pain and frustration. Mom and Dra mostly carried on with whatever they were doing: vacuuming, folding clothes, making dinner. No one coddled me or kept me company. They felt sorry for me, of course. Who wanted to see their little girl suffer? But I guess they figured that other than giving me generous servings of castor oil, there wasn't much else to be done. When I had hernia surgery at age five, I took the hit like one of those wrestlers we watched on television and moved on.

The women in my family were warriors, without ever seeing themselves that way. Just as our ancestors and forebears had survived centuries of oppression and brutality by shoring up their defenses to the thousandth degree, so too did Mom and Dra behave exactly as they were expected to: without sentimentality or the slightest hint of fragility. They meant us no harm. In fact, cultivating our strength was their way of equipping us for battle, just as their forebears had done for them.

For years, I did my best to absorb the lessons they conveyed. Even today, I do a pretty good imitation of a strong Black woman when the situation calls for it. In fact, part of me *is* that woman. But there's a bigger part, I think, that never quite embraced that narrative. Barely hidden beneath my thick skin, an unspoken desire flickered on. The odds weren't in my favor, I knew that. But my heart was resolute. If I listened to it closely, it would prove to be my most powerful resource. I might have to reject everything Mom and Dra taught me about being a strong Black woman in order to heal the broken parts of myself. But that was OK. I decided I was willing to pay that price.

I imagined that I might one day have the kind of dream family I saw on television, with mothers and fathers who sweet-talked and played with their children. I know now that families are *not* perfect, of course. Black families like my own are often laden with generational trauma. But back then, I was convinced that if I wished for it hard enough, my father would come back. And if he came back, maybe my mother would smile and tickle and kiss me too, just like those happy moms and dads on television. I would have the family of my dreams, I vowed in some quiet corner of my being: a family that felt whole, with no one missing. I *would* have my happily ever after.

uncle mervin

"Did you brush your teeth?" Mom asked. We were warm and cozy under a freshly laundered chenille bedspread. For a special treat, and because it was Valentine's Day, Mom had let me eat Fig Newtons and stay up past my bedtime so that we could watch *Hawaii Five-O* together. We were like "two bugs in a rug," she said. A rare treat indeed.

Usually, I brushed my teeth like clockwork. I was a good girl who did pretty much everything Mom and Dra asked without complaint. But it was nearly eleven o' clock and I was just too tired. Instead, I ran the toothbrush under the water and placed it back in the cup. "Zookie?" My eyes were closed, but I could hear Mom smiling. "Did you *really* brush your teeth?" *How did she know? Ugh.* Off I trudged, back to the bathroom to finish the job.

Dra and Lisa were asleep at the back of the apartment when we heard a sudden knock. Ours was a tranquil, residential neighborhood. With the television off, and the shooting and car chases done, the house was silent. We had no dog or cat. Not even a hamster to spin around on a wheel. It was just us. Mom and I exchanged confused looks. We weren't the kind of family that got visitors even during daytime hours. Mom and Dra didn't have casual girlfriends or chatty neighborhood acquaintances. In those early years, they mostly kept to themselves.

Mom padded into the living room with me tracking close behind. I pressed myself behind her legs as she studied the peephole. Slowly, with impending dread, she opened the door.

"Is this the home of Mervin Brent?" I felt my mother crumple beside me.

She stared back at two uniformed police officers. "I'm his sister."

My uncle Mervin had trafficked marijuana from Tijuana to Los Angeles for some time to support his heroin addiction. He was good at it. Until he wasn't. He got caught and was sent away to a minimum-security prison. After he got out, he met Jane, a soft-spoken Texan with porcelain skin. I remember that she drove a burgundy Cadillac and sang along to easy hits on the radio. The night they met, she and my uncle sat up together all night on a bench at Venice Beach, talking.

Jane was different, as Mom would later explain. She had absolutely no experience with drugs or drug dealers. With her in his life, Mervin turned a corner. He checked himself into a rehabilitation program at UCLA and got clean. He signed up for job training as a welder and, before long, he was earning a legal paycheck. He was spending more time with us girls lately, too, taking us to lunch at IHOP, which, for me, was nothing short of a five-star restaurant. I couldn't have been happier with my banana nut pancakes, with thick chunks of butter and maple syrup.

Even Ms. Honda at our day-care center called Mervin "sweet" and "winsome" when he came to pick us up. He sat in the big armchair by the door when he visited, regaling us with silly stories and anecdotes. I remember how he'd throw his head back and release the most enormous belly laugh I'd ever heard. His presence, even amid his battle with addiction, was more than we could say for that of Lisa's mother.

One of the officers asked, "Is there a man of the house?"

Dra joined us then, tightening her robe. "What is this concerning?"

"Ma'am." He nodded. The officer's tone was surprisingly gentle. Mom would later wonder if he was uncomfortable delivering his news to two women and a small child.

"I'm sorry to inform you. This is concerning the death of Mervin Brent."

"Oh!" Mom turned to me, desolate.

My grandmother caught herself against a wall. "Lord have mercy."

The officer paused long enough for them to find their bearings. "The cause of death appears to have been a drug overdose. Heroin."

When she finally spoke, Mom's voice was thick with emotion. "Where is he?"

The officer glanced at his notes. "His body was found in a vacant drug house at . . . 562 North Serrano Avenue."

To this day, Mom can still recite the address from memory. I wonder how many times she'd gone over it in her mind. Uncle Mervin's attempts to get clean had come too late, she would later say. He just "slid back."

While we stood frozen at the door, Lisa slept peacefully in her bed, unaware of how her life was about to change. Later, she would tell me how strange it had been. At that moment, she'd been dreaming of her father, and it was, as she described it, one of the happiest dreams of her life. In fact, I never believed it was a dream at all. It was her father, I decided, coming to spend his last moments at her side. No doubt, he wanted to surround his precious girl, his only child, with the love he now glimpsed. I believe Lisa must have felt that blinding white light too.

After Mervin's death, my mother closed the door to our bedroom most days and stayed there for what felt like hours, sobbing over her tarot cards. Arranging symbols across our bed, she studied the images and then shuffled and tried again. We didn't have a stereo, so Mom used my plastic kid's turntable to play a 45 single of Frank Sinatra's "My Way," over and over again. It was her ode to Mervin, their shared swan song of defeat.

What I didn't know then was that during all those hours sequestered in our bedroom, Mom was not only mourning her brother; she was also grieving the loss of her own innocence. She must have realized by then that my father, a drug addict and alcoholic, was also well and truly gone. She would be a single mother after all. Mom's brother, grandfather, and a host of other family members were addicted to drugs or alcohol or both. Dra believed that we had been cursed as a family. Perhaps, at that point, Mom was starting to agree.

Preheat oven to 450 degrees. Rub cooking oil over potatoes. Poke holes with a fork and wrap in aluminum foil. Bake for thirty minutes.

Mom was famous for leaving us girls to-do lists. She printed them neatly on white index cards, using extra-fine felt-tip pens. Lisa and I did our chores and waited in front of the television. Finally, around sundown, Mom emerged from our bedroom red-eyed and droopy.

During normal, everyday exchanges at the grocery store or the bank, I would often search her face as she interacted with the cashier or the teller. No matter how cheerful the person standing before her ("Thank you for shopping at Lucky's!"), my mother never reciprocated. She was polite, but a soft-spoken "thank you" seemed to be her emotional limit. In the streets, I rarely saw her remove her sunglasses, and during those early years of my life, it seemed to me that she almost never smiled. She didn't date or see friends during those years. She worked, came home, and locked herself in the bedroom with her tarot cards.

"What's wrong, Mommy?"

She sighed, tears welling.

"Are you sad?"

Mom nodded.

I reached for her hand. "Can I help you?"

She shook her head.

I had no idea how to fix what was wrong. Whatever small bits of herself she could give me over the years, I cherished like precious jewels on a necklace I prayed would not break. Like the time we'd sat alone on the wooden floor of our first apartment, singing along with Mister Rogers. *You are my friend, you are special.* But now I had to wonder. Was I still her friend? Was I still special?

Mom stood up straight, as if suddenly remembering her responsibilities.

"Your sweater. Do you remember when you last had it?"

My stomach dropped. "No."

I had been going through a disturbing phase. Every day, Mom sent me to school with a sweater or a light jacket for the mild California winter, and every day, I came home empty-handed. I abandoned my clothes on the playground, on the school bus, at the candy store. Anywhere and everywhere. No one knew why. Least of all me.

"You don't have any idea where you left it?"

I shook my head.

Mom looked away. There was barely enough money for rent and food, much less new clothes.

A thought occurred to me then. I stared into Mom's eyes, hoping for a connection. "I still have my poncho!" A festive, sunflower yellow, it was my all-time favorite—a classic 1970s knit pattern, complete with fringes and pom-pom balls. When I spun around in my poncho, it felt like I was wearing a celebration. Yellow meant pushing the bad things away and focusing single-mindedly on the good. It was more than a piece of clothing. It was my worldview.

For many years, in fact, my memory of myself was just that: a happy little girl twirling in circles on the playground and posing for the camera in that poncho. It wasn't until much later that I allowed myself to consider the possibility that perhaps my childhood might not have been as sunny as I'd imagined. Maybe I *hadn't* lost all those jackets and sweaters by accident. Maybe I was trying to get my mother's attention. Maybe losing those clothes was my way of crying out. But I never could seem to get Mom's attention. Not then, and not later.

We were a house of single, working women and girls with not a single husband, father, grandfather, brother, or uncle in sight. Fernando Noche, who lived not three feet away, across the hallway, must have known this. And with that knowledge, he inched closer to his prey.

noches

"Wanna play dolls?" I pestered Lisa until she was beside herself with annoyance. "Do you?"

She stared at the television. "No!"

"What about house? Wanna play house?"

No answer. *The Jetsons* was on, one of her favorite shows.

"Secretary?" I persisted. Mom had brought some of those pink "While You Were Out" message pads home from her secretarial job. I placed them in front of Lisa. "You can be the boss. Come on. Pleeeeeeease?"

Every now and again, I could entice her, but mostly she preferred to be left alone. At ten, she seemed to have more important things on her mind than playing make-believe. Though she was never one to complain as a child, the confusion of her situation eventually became too much, even for her. When *The Jetsons* was over, she left the room and headed for the kitchen table where Mom and Dra sat talking and smoking.

I followed.

"Where's my mommy?" she asked.

Mom and Dra exchanged helpless glances. Lisa's mother, an alcoholic, had brought her to Dra's door as a baby and never come back. "What do you mean?" Dra tried to make light of it. "*We're* your mommy, of course!" But Lisa wasn't having it. "No. I mean the mommy whose stomach I came out of."

Mom stood up, lighting the oven for chicken potpies.

Lisa needed answers, but they had none to give.

Most days, we went across the hall to visit our neighbors, the Noches, who had three small boys under the age of six. But it wasn't them that we went to see. In fact, we found them quite annoying, especially the eldest, who made constant, overtly sexual gestures. Our friend was Lina, Mrs. Noche's sixteen-year-old sister, who served as a live-in nanny and housekeeper. Modest and shy, Lina alternated between the same two sets of Kmart polyester outfits, clipping her hair off her face while she worked. She wasn't allowed to socialize with friends her own age. Lisa and I were all she had. So we sat at the Noches' kitchen table, chatting with Lina as she soaped dishes.

"But why can't we go to the movies?" I whined.

"Because they need me here." Lina's voice was soft, with a hint of an accent.

"It's not fair." I glanced at Lisa, who nodded her agreement.

I didn't think of Fernando Noche, Lina's brother-in-law, as a particularly nice man. He was surly, often slinking into his bedroom and closing the door without a word to anyone. Once, when Lina dared to announce that she wanted to go on a date, he responded by smashing a television set through the living room window, shattering it across the driveway. None of us saw this as a red flag, apparently.

To me, he was one of the few examples I had of a father—one who was there, in the house, day after day. For that fact alone, he'd earned my implicit respect, outweighing any hesitation I may have had about his character. The Noches were a real family, it seemed to me. Something I longed for desperately.

"Can we spend the night at Lina's tonight?" I asked Mom.

"OK." She answered without fanfare, her mind on other things.

Lisa and I did a little cheer, gathering up sleeping bags and pillows and carrying them across the hall. We laid out our gear camping-style, on the floor of the bedroom that Lina shared with the boys. We told ghost stories and jokes, and before long, we were all asleep.

What happened next remains a mystery to me, even today. Somehow, I was left alone in the apartment with Fernando. How or why, I have no idea. As an adult I would later probe my family for answers. Lisa speculated that maybe she went to church with Lina and the other family members the next morning, an unlikely explanation. Why would the entire Noche family have gone to church without me? And the idea that Lisa, my fearless protector, would have left me alone—or that Mom and Dra would have allowed this—was equally implausible. It made no sense. What was even more frustrating was that no one seemed to remember much of anything. Revisiting the past only left me with more questions.

But here's what I do know.

I know that I awoke the next morning to find bright sunshine streaming across the room and Fernando Noche crawling toward me on his hands and knees. I didn't understand the words he spoke, but I knew that something was wrong.

"Ven acá."

"No."

I pushed myself backward across the forest green shag carpet, causing my long flannel nightgown to spark with friction.

Fernando crawled closer. "Ven."

I began to cry. "No."

I saw his hands up close, perhaps for the first time. They were rough, calloused. Working hands. They found their way to my vulva. I remember nothing else about the assault, although I believe that at some point, I must have fled to the bathroom. The reason I know this is because, for the next three decades, I was haunted by nightmares in which I was always fleeing, running from someone or something, and taking refuge in bathrooms. A bathroom was involved in Fernando's assault somehow. Of this, I was sure.

There is a related incident that haunts my memory as well.

A few days, weeks, or maybe months later, I remember Mom and Dra bustling back and forth in our apartment. They were worked up about something, rustling around in a kind of whispered frenzy. They wet towels with soap, pulled items from cabinets. Apparently either Lisa or me—no one seems to remember which; I think it was Lisa, she thinks it was me— had gotten her first period. "But she's too young," the grown-ups protested in hushed tones. And they were right. We were too young.

In the end, the "period" turned out to be a false alarm, which was even more troubling. Years later, neither Mom nor Dra could explain to me why one of us girls might have suddenly bled for no reason and then stopped. The mind is a miraculous thing, as I would later learn. It knows exactly how much we can take and how much to submerge and hide. Our entire family had cultivated a habit of losing time. In later conversations with one another, we often found that large chunks of important memories were simply gone, buried in a place where they could not hurt us.

laurel canyon

Tom Mack was on the phone. "It's going to be a hot day," he told Mom. "Why don't you and Christine bring the girls over for a swim?" Tom scored and produced music for hit movies such as *The Godfather*, *Rosemary's Baby*, and *Willy Wonka & the Chocolate Factory*, as well as the original 1966 television series *Mission: Impossible*. He had a sprawling wooden ranch house at the top of West Crescent Drive with a stunning view of Hollywood.

A swim? At a house?

Strutting like we'd just won the lottery, Lisa, Mom, Dra, and I piled into the Corolla, prepared to make the steep ascent into the celebrity-dotted hills of Laurel Canyon. Seals and Crofts' "Summer Breeze" played on the radio as Lisa and I stuck our heads out the window, laughing into the humid air. Mom must have been terrified as we ascended higher and higher, the Corolla barely gripping the edges of the canyon roads. There were blind curves and a path so narrow that if two cars met along the way, one would have to go into reverse so the other could pass. As anxious as we all must have been (Dra pressing her foot into the passenger-side floor mat again and again), none of us could hide our excitement.

"What's that smell?" Garlic and onions wafted toward us from the kitchen when we arrived.

"Linguini with clam sauce." Tom winked, stooping to give me a hug. At six foot three, he was a striking figure, with white hair and a Santa Claus–thick white beard, to which he added white slacks and white tennis shoes. In true 1970s form, he topped the look off with a paisley silk shirt, unbuttoned to reveal a swath of white chest hair. I remember a comment that Mom once made in an offhanded way. Even in his sixties, she noted in passing, Tom was "elegant." Some years earlier, he had married Mom's closest childhood friend from Chicago. The ceremony took place in that same house, with the bride and groom exchanging vows on the pool deck. The marriage didn't last. Mom's friend eventually went back to her first husband, leaving Tom once again on his own.

Lisa and I changed into swimsuits while Tom passed Mom and Dra cold beers on the couch. Our visits to Laurel Canyon gave them a chance to relax for what felt like the first time in a while. Out of the bathroom in record time, Lisa and I were making a dash for the diving board when Tom stunned us with a question.

"Hey, Lisa? Kristal? How would you girls like to go to Disneyland?"

Screeeeeeech. We stopped cold in our tracks like characters in one of those Road Runner cartoons. *Did he say Disneyland?* Too stunned even to respond, we looked to Mom and Dra for a reaction.

"I don't see why not," Mom said, looking as flabbergasted as we felt.

"Yay!" We shrieked, exploding into Olympian leaps and stunts.

"OK then," Tom said, laughing. "It's a deal!"

Clearly, he adored my mother, and I suspect that the feeling was mutual. Why no romance ever developed between them remained just one more of my mother's mysteries—thoughts and feelings that she kept closely guarded, sharing with no one. Mom was so emotionally aloof, so deeply private, in fact, that one could easily mistake her reserve for indifference. That was certainly the case for me.

If I had been abandoned and betrayed by men in the past, Tom Mack represented the first enduring and stable presence of a loving male figure in my young life. His contribution was stunning in its simplicity, and yet, it had the power to transform our family completely. That he was an older white man from a culture entirely foreign to us was part of the beauty of our connection. Our differences only made the bond more meaningful. To add to that, Mom and Dra were also, perhaps unwittingly, laying the groundwork for Lisa and me to expand our own possibilities, to see beyond our current economic standing, in what scholars and researchers would later confirm is one of the most powerful indicators for escaping poverty: friendships across class lines.

Then, in October 1976, when I was eleven years old, another white-haired man came into our lives. Frank Ashe wore wire-rimmed glasses and the expression of an intellectual. The first time we visited his Laurel Canyon home—just down the road from Tom's house—Lisa and I tentatively stepped inside.

"Why don't you take a look up there?" Frank gestured toward a staircase off the front-door entrance. Lisa and I glanced at one another and darted upstairs.

"Whoa!" we called out in amazement once we reached the top. There, completely secluded from the rest of the house, were two side-by-side miniature bedrooms—the same rooms that had once belonged to Frank's own daughters. We raced back and forth between them, each time discovering a new hidden cubbyhole or secret closet along the way. The rooms were so whimsical, it was as if they'd been designed by a magical fairy elf.

Mom and Frank joined us on the landing between the rooms.

"How would you like to live here?" he asked.

They'd met at one of Tom's Halloween parties, where Mom had gone dressed up as an alien. At fifty-four, Frank, a screenwriter and author, was more than two decades Mom's senior, with pasty skin and thinning hair. They enjoyed going to jazz clubs and bars together, and out to dinner at the Mulholland Tennis Club, where Frank was a founding member. Frank knew the answer to any question you could think of, which I'm sure my cerebral mother admired. Whatever obscure topic Lisa or I might come up with to try and stump him, he knew all about it, delivering an encyclopedia-like dissertation that left us itching to go back to playing.

"Would these be *our* rooms?" Lisa wanted to know.

Frank nodded. "You can paint them any color you like."

I studied him more closely to make sure I'd heard correctly. Our low-rent apartments had always been painted regulation white and off-white. I never knew that a home could be anything but beige.

"Any color?" I shrieked. "My room is going to be yellow! And orange! And red! The colors of the sun!" I tugged at Lisa's arm, dancing a jig. "What color is yours going to be?" She shrugged but I could see by the upturn of her lips that she was as excited as I was.

We must have stayed up there for a solid hour that afternoon, inspecting every corner of our new rooms. I ran my hand across the sloping plywood ceiling, which gave each of the mirror-image rooms a triangular, attic-like shape. Winding metal hand cranks, I opened windows to the east and west to survey the views. A low-hanging eucalyptus tree obscured the front of the house, and just beneath my window, I spotted a private courtyard area. It would soon become my favorite place in the world, a refuge for making mud pies and inventing solitary games in the quiet shade.

Life in Laurel Canyon was different from anything we'd ever known before. Suddenly, we were surrounded by whiteness, wealth, and celebrity. Our schoolmates were child actors from television shows and movies. Friends of the Beach Boys. Friends of the Jackson 5. The sons and the daughters of directors, cinematographers, and Grammy Award–winning musicians. We ran into child actor Quinn Cummings regularly at the Mulholland Tennis Club. She'd been nominated for an Oscar for her role as Lucy in *The Goodbye Girl*. To us, she represented a kind of girlish royalty.

And then, there we were: two biracial girls who, no matter how hard we tried, simply could not get our frizzy, poufy hair to lie flat on our heads. It is difficult to describe the feeling of knowing that you are not beautiful—at least, not in that classic way that everyone celebrated—for reasons that no one has ever quite explained to you. You simply sense that beauty is something *out there*, reserved for those with white skin and hair that blows in the wind. I'd grasped this truth from a young age, and life in Laurel Canyon only solidified my beliefs.

Of the four of us, Dra was the only truly brown-skinned woman in our family. I sometimes wonder what she made of our family's sudden star-studded existence in the nearly all-white Hollywood Hills. In any case, it was a question she would never answer. For reasons neither Lisa nor

I could have understood at the time, Dra was not invited to live with us on Wonderland Avenue. For the first time in our young lives, our grandmother was not in the next room, across the hall, or down the street. Being apart from her felt strange. I wondered if it also felt strange to Mom.

But apparently, Mom felt only relief. It was her first real taste of independence, and she reveled in it, relieved to finally have some distance from her mother, the person who, to her mind, had both supported and suffocated her.

dra

While Mom settled into a new beginning with Frank, Dra was also busy rearranging her own life. She rented a single apartment in Century City, which Lisa and I wholeheartedly approved of, since it was within walking distance of both See's Candies and Gelson's market, which had the best brownies we'd ever tasted. We especially loved to do gymnastics in the back lot, behind the apartment building. Hanging off a clothing line, we pretended to be Nadia Comăneci, who, at the 1976 Olympic Games and at the age of just fourteen, became the first gymnast to receive a perfect 10.0 score, inspiring girls all around the world.

More importantly, we could see that Dra was happy there. After decades of caring for her children and grandchildren, she was finally free to relax and enjoy a bit of leisure time in her own home. She even had a new boyfriend, Robert Ware, whom I had liked from the instant I met him. Still in her early fifties, Dra faced the prospect of a new beginning. Robert was serious about her, and before long he would propose marriage. He was predictable, in a comforting way that none of us had ever quite seen before.

"How's my big girl?" Dra took hold of Lisa's head with both hands one Saturday afternoon when Mom dropped us off for a weekend visit. She turned to me next, planting a brusque kiss on my cheek. I didn't realize how terribly I'd missed her until that moment, when she squeezed my hand just a little more tightly than usual. Robert also broke into a wide smile at the sight of us, crouching down to our level for a proper greeting. "Hey there, now! What's kickin', my little chickens?"

They fed us bologna sandwiches, coleslaw, and potato chips for lunch at Dra's small kitchen nook. Then, after we'd eaten, Robert set up a folding card table in the living room.

"Pick your poison." He directed this to me, since I was the one who loved games.

"Dominoes!"

Robert threw me a doubtful, teasing look. "Oh, so you think you can beat me, huh? All right. Well. We'll just have to see about that." We arranged the blocks on the table, while Lisa stretched out to watch television.

Seconds later, I slapped down a six-three, placing it next to Robert's double-six. "Fifteen," I said, gloating.

"Uh-oh." Dra recorded my points onto a notepad.

"I see, said the blind man." Robert stared at me with mock seriousness. He always recited the same line whenever I made a good play, adding, "to his deaf dog." Knitting his eyebrows together, he would ponder the tiles with exaggerated concern. "I see," he repeated, as though genuinely stumped. "I see . . . I see."

"Oh, go on and play," Dra teased. "If you even got anything in all that mess."

As an adult, I have often wondered how our lives might have been different had Dra decided to take a leap of faith and become Robert's wife. I wonder what it might have meant for us girls to watch her grow old in a mature relationship with a loving Black man. I wonder what it might have meant for us to be given the opportunity to embrace a grandfather figure. I wonder what neurosynaptic brain connections might have been rewired, revolutionized, had we had the chance to love, and be loved by, Robert Ware.

But it was not meant to be.

As it turned out, fate had molded and shaped our family circumstances long before I was born, in a place far away, during an era paved by both bliss and tragedy. It was our destiny, it seemed, to remain a house of women and girls.

I have only ever seen one picture of my two uncles together. It's a Polaroid snapshot. In it, my uncle Arthur, whom we saw rarely, leaned into my uncle Mervin as they walked, chuckling over some inside joke. Clowning just a little. They were tall and handsome in their twenties. Fit, with neat, medium-sized Afros. They looked at the ground or off into the distance, unaware of the camera. Just two cool dudes in oversize sunglasses and bell-bottoms. These were the men in our lives, such as they were. Absent. Unknown.

I loved to hear stories about my grandparents back in the day, with their drinking and gambling and Chicago rent parties. They were Deep South transplants—from a pin-drop town called Moscow, which was just east of Pine Bluff, the smallest town in Arkansas. My grandmother left with her father when she was still a girl, joining the Great Migration, which saw six million African Americans escape Jim Crow between 1915 and 1970. From that day forward, if anyone asked Dra where she was from, she would say Chicago. As if Arkansas had never existed.

Chicago was where she met my grandfather, Arthur Sr., who had lost both of his parents at a young age. At fifteen, finding himself no longer welcome in the home of an uncle, he found work on a nearby farm in exchange for room and board. As it turned out, that farm happened to belong to Dra's grandmother, Miss Penny.

"Who's that girl, Miss Penny?"

One evening after dinner, Arthur pointed to a picture of Dra on the mantel. At fifteen, she was about his same age.

"That's Christine," my great-grandmother told him. "She went up to Chicago with her daddy."

"That so? When?" He was a plucky young man, handsome and confident.

"Oh, round about eight years now. She left here when she was a girl."

"Well, Miss Penny," declared my grandfather, "I'm gonna go up there and marry your granddaughter." And that's just what he did. Arthur Sr.

took a train to Chicago, where he met my grandmother and married her shortly thereafter. Their first child, my uncle Arthur Jr., was born when Dra was just seventeen years old.

Up north, my grandparents did some hard living, smoking Old Golds and Herbert Tareytons and drinking whiskey. Dra even dipped snuff, chewing it up and spitting it out like the men. She had a hand in the illegal numbers game, too, secretly taking bets in a vacant apartment. They drank and gambled on the weekends; worked hard; fought and partied. That was life on the South Side.

My great-grandfather, Willie Long, who lived next door with his wife, was a "falling-down alcoholic"—as Dra once described him to me—who dragged Dra around as a girl to houses that sold bootleg whiskey. He'd get drunk on the weekends and come home at all hours of the night. "Here," he'd say, tossing a package of gum at Dra and her half sister. He may have been a drunk, Dra explained to me, but he never came home empty-handed without a treat for his children. Dra knew that her daddy loved her, she said. That was never even a question.

Willie wasn't the only alcoholic. So, too, was Dra's uncle and, later, her half sister, who died of cirrhosis of the liver before the age of forty. There was a time when I guess some might have even put that label on my grandmother, although it wouldn't have been accurate, since she could, and often did, stop drinking for long stretches of time whenever the spirit moved her to do so. Mostly, she and her husband worked during the week and let loose on the weekends with friends, playing cards and dancing.

Yet, when I imagine my grandparents' life in Chicago, it is always deeply colored by dysfunction and tragedy: booze, poverty, infidelity, betrayal, addiction, and, most of all, two specific instances of devastating violence.

These were two events that have always stood out among our family lore. Life-changing traumas that would alter my grandmother's worldview forever, and therefore my mother's, and mine and Lisa's too. Living in the aftermath of these violent acts shaped us all into the women we would become, whether we knew it or not. It would not be an exaggeration to say that my grandmother's past in Chicago had a hand in sealing our own fate. We may not have known exactly how, or why, but because of her history, we were all destined, it seemed, to a life in which men were not to be trusted and women were better off alone.

hollywood boulevard

Mom had dark circles under her eyes and looked as forlorn as I felt. She had left Frank, whom I gathered she respected but perhaps never quite managed to fall in love with. After less than two years, our dollhouse, Frank's miniature toy castle at the top of Wonderland Avenue, was gone.

In its place, Mom rented a two-bedroom apartment in a sagging building on Hollywood Boulevard. "It's only temporary," she told us, the look on her face reflecting our own disappointment as we surveyed the building's chipped paint. Lisa and I did our best to overlook the rundown, faded feel of our new surroundings as we unloaded cardboard boxes and lugged them to the garage elevator.

"I'll go park the car," she told us. "Wait here."

"It's not so bad," I offered to Lisa, plunking myself down on a box as we waited for the elevator. When it arrived, a petite young woman who couldn't have been more than nineteen stepped out.

"Hello." She had long, blond hair. The kind Lisa and I secretly envied. We nodded. "Hi."

As she bounced away, we studied each other's faces, puzzling over the same question.

"Wasn't that . . . ?"

"Yeah! It totally was."

Lisa flipped the emergency switch. We covered our ears against its ringing and hoisted boxes inside.

"Mom!" I called across the garage. "The elevator's here!"

"We just saw that girl from *Dallas*!" I sang out as Mom came hiking up the sloping garage driveway. Chug went the elevator, bumping along to the third floor.

"Oh really?" Mom must have cared as much about Charlene Tilton in that moment as she did about a rock. But for us, the celebrity's presence in our building was a spark in an otherwise dismal landscape. Later, we would learn that Belinda Carlisle of the Go-Go's also lived there. That was the Hollywood of my youth—aspiring rockers carting their guitars up and down Sunset Boulevard and wannabe starlets living in dumpy apartments, waiting for their big break. To the rest of the world, it was a city where fantasies came true. Tourists rarely saw behind the curtain to the realities of pimps, prostitutes, and psychopaths strategically positioned on every corner.

In truth, Hollywood was a place of indescribable danger. Once there, I learned quickly how to emit an air of thick-skinned toughness when I was out in the streets. The trick was to walk fast, eyes straight ahead and shoulders rigid. Most of the time, my rugged persona worked, warding off the predators. But not always.

One Saturday afternoon, I was walking home from a friend's house in Laurel Canyon when a man pulled into a driveway ahead, blocking my path.

"Hi there! You're very pretty."

I circumvented his car, continuing along the sidewalk.

"I was wondering if you'd like a job as a model?" he called out through the driver's side window.

Hmm, I thought. This was new.

"I work for the Sears catalog. We're looking for girls your age."

I leaned in slightly for a better look. He was a clean-cut young man in a polo shirt. White.

"A job?"

"Yeah. It pays really well. Fifteen dollars an hour, and you get to keep the clothes."

He had me at *job*.

"Get in," he offered.

I slid into the passenger seat.

"Now . . ." He reached casually for a pen and piece of paper. "What's your name?"

I gave it to him without a moment's hesitation.

"Phone number?"

Gave him that too.

"And . . . where do you live?"

"Just down the street." Luckily, being new to the neighborhood, I hadn't quite memorized the address.

"That's OK. What time do your parents come home from work?"

"It's just my mom," I confessed, spilling out everything except the size of my training bra. "About six thirty."

He nodded as though completing a checklist and tucked his notes into the glove box. Then he proceeded to unzip his pants and pull his penis out.

"Sorry. I have this medical condition and I have to put cream on it every few hours or else I'll be in a lot of pain." He reached for a tube of white lotion and squirted. "Can you help me?" I may have been gullible, but I wasn't stupid. Flinging open the passenger door, I mumbled good-bye and hightailed it out of there.

Still, despite the strangeness of the encounter, I honestly believed my life was about to change. I was runway bound! I was going to be a model for Sears! When Mom came home from work, I told her all about my new job offer—leaving out the part about the penis and the medical condition, of course. "And I get to keep the clothes!" I concluded.

Mom stared at me. Her tight-lipped expression was not exactly the reaction I'd expected. "Did you give him our address?" For the first time, the thought occurred to me that maybe I had done something wrong.

"No."

Mom weighed this carefully. "Did he touch you? Did he hurt you in any way?"

"No."

Now I was getting scared. Mom took a drag of her cigarette. "Did you get his name? Or his license plate number?"

I shook my head.

"Then we have no way to report him to the police."

Tears welled in my eyes. Somehow, I had disappointed her, and that fact hurt more than anything else. Mom turned to me, her face contorted in anger. "Don't you ever get in a strange man's car again. Do you understand?" I nodded, feeling sad, ashamed, and confused. Clearly, I had done something wrong. What it was, though, I couldn't exactly say.

That wasn't the only time I would be sexually harassed in the streets of Hollywood. Far from it. Men of all stripes threatened and intimidated me as a preteen and adolescent. At times, the Black men who did so came for me in a highly racialized way. There was one pimp in particular who was a regular fixture in our neighborhood. He slunk behind me with pink rollers in his processed hair, catcalling as I walked down the street.

At fourteen, when I was on my way to work at a tourist shop on Hollywood Boulevard, he became especially aggressive. (I had lied on the application and said I was sixteen to get the job.) I did my best to ignore him, rolling my eyes in an exaggerated show of disgust, but that only caused him to ramp up his attack. "Oh! It's like that, huh?" He stepped up his pace, inching closer. "So now you too good to speak, High Yella?"

I was speed-walking now, while trying to maintain a nonchalant demeanor.

"Answer me, bitch! You think you too good for me?"

I turned a couple of sharp corners and ducked into a glitzy apartment building, pretending I lived there. Yeah, I was too good for him, I thought once I'd caught my breath. But not because I was light-skinned. *Because he was a pimp.*

Other than these episodes, Lisa and I settled into Hollywood Boulevard fairly well. We rearranged stuffed animals on our twin beds and retaped *Baretta* and *Starsky and Hutch* posters onto the walls—at least, that's what I put up on my side. Already we were beginning to drift apart in our likes and dislikes, and Lisa's side of the room fell more in line with the rock and roll lifestyle she was beginning to emulate. She plastered images of sweaty, shirtless Robert Plant and Steven Tyler on the wall, their lips caressing the microphone at live concerts. Before long, I would follow her lead, as was usually the case when it came to Lisa.

We were a family of girls and women again, and secretly I was relieved. No matter how good Frank had been to us, there had always been a nagging doubt in the back of my mind. Quietly, and without a word to anyone about it, I firmly believed that one day he would "try something" with me or Lisa, causing our dollhouse existence to come crashing down. It was inevitable. Men could not be trusted. They left. They died. They hurt you. You could take that to the bank.

I have since wondered if Mom and Dra might have been relieved too.

Robert Ware had proposed to Dra, but she turned him down. Instead, she left her Century City apartment and moved into a building directly across the street from us, coming to the aid of her children and grandchildren once again, just as she'd always done. Although she was not yet sixty and would live a healthy life for many years to come, her love affair with Robert Ware would be her last meaningful relationship with a man.

Dra carried on working as a housekeeper for the Mendel family, a wealthy Jewish lawyer husband and homemaker wife with three young daughters in the Pacific Palisades. She rode the bus more than an hour each way, transferring twice, to get to their sprawling coastal home. She and Janet Mendel formed a friendship, and it was Mrs. Mendel, as Dra insisted on calling her, who made sure that at ages ten and eleven, Lisa and I enrolled at the Center for Enriched Studies middle school, the first magnet school in Los Angeles and also the first school in the district to be created as part of its voluntary integration program.

At the end of Dra's long days at the Mendel home, she sometimes stopped at Ralph's grocery store on Sunset Boulevard, carting heavy bags uphill. On those afternoons, she would pass the Temple Israel playground (where she would, oddly, later secure a babysitting job for me, her Christian granddaughter). She nodded across the fence at the women wearing long skirts and dark wigs.

Sometimes Dra would muse about the way Jewish women always seemed to come to her aid, even back in segregated Chicago, where Mrs. Goldsmith, a Jewish homemaker, believed in her enough to make Dra manager of her and her husband's apartment building, the Peer Manor Apartments. That move allowed my grandparents to leave their one-room apartment at Thirtieth Street and Prairie Avenue and relocate to Hyde Park, where my seven-year-old mother, who had slept in a living room chair for most of her life, now had her first bed.

There had always been pivotal white women in Dra's life, it seemed.

In Chicago, she cleaned house for Mrs. Ditkovsky, who took Dra to her first opera and treated her children to their first circus. Women helping women. It was a theme that would be forever ingrained in our consciousness.

There was a mystique about white people in my grandmother's view, too, something she herself could never quite attain. Her husband's father, my great-grandfather, had been a white landowner in Arkansas, and Dra believed that mix of genetic history affected how my grandfather carried himself. He had a kind of assurance as he moved about in the world, she once told me. I remember her expression as she said it, as though she were trying to decipher a great mystery. George, a man Dra dated briefly, was mixed race too, of Italian and Black ancestry, and to her, he carried that same mystique. It made sense that two of Dra's three children would end up with white partners and have biracial children. In some deep part of herself, she may have believed the old axiom, *If you're Black, get back. If you're white, you're alright.*

7

rockin' out

At Bancroft Junior High, I fell for a boy who was like me: neither Black nor white, but somewhere in between. Saul had another thing going for him too. He was a real-life aspiring guitarist. As Lisa and I now fashioned ourselves into something of miniature rock and roll groupies, he was perfect. But Saul was painfully shy, with thick, curly hair that completely covered his forehead and eyes, as if he wanted nothing more than to fade out of view. Since I was also shy, and deeply insecure, there wasn't much to our conversations.

"I like your hair," I offered during recess.

He grinned. "I like yours too."

We were at the food truck, where kids smoked cigarettes between classes. Saul's friend Steven Adler, who played drums, was flirting with Lisa, asking if she was going to the beach that weekend. Lisa wasn't interested, though. She had her eye on a red-haired dude who hung out with the *vatos*.

"Well. See you." I blushed at Saul.

"Yeah. See you."

"He likes you," Lisa noted as we turned to leave.

I let out a giddy, nervous laugh. "No, he doesn't."

"Yes, he does. He gets all googly-eyed whenever you're around."

I hoped she was right. In my imagination, Saul and I were the perfect match. Both of us biracial. Both with Black moms. And he was a genuine rocker too? What more could a girl ask for? It was still too early for Prince or Lenny Kravitz, and Lisa and I weren't sophisticated enough to know about Jimi Hendrix. So, there we were. Two biracial teenagers embracing a nearly all-white rock and roll universe.

This led to some awkward encounters, to say the least.

Like the time we rushed over to Peaches Records on Hollywood Boulevard, hoping for a signed copy of Ted Nugent's new album and to meet "the Nuge" in person. When we finally made it to the front of the line several hours later, "Terrible Ted" stunned me by planting a kiss squarely on my lips. He kissed Lisa too, which sent her shrieking down the aisle with joy. Of course, we knew nothing about his racist beliefs back then, and it would be years before he'd be widely lambasted for his comments about slain teenager Trayvon Martin, in addition to a slew of other disturbing remarks about Black people.

Still, at that time, something about the music and the rock and roll culture attracted us. Already, we'd amassed a drawerful of concert stubs. We'd seen the Cars, the Babys, the Who, the Boomtown Rats, Aerosmith, and Tom Petty, although we couldn't help but notice the scant number of Black people at these venues, which we registered in a kind of sideways peripheral vision. It certainly needled us when the white girls bent over and flipped their long hair and when they laughed in that carefree way they had. I couldn't deny that we were outsiders in this terrain.

Years later I would watch a documentary about Lynyrd Skynyrd and wonder: Did we even notice they flew the Confederate flag as we belted out the lyrics to "Free Bird"? And yet, even in retrospect, I couldn't help but marvel at their artistic brilliance—how they holed up at that cabin, fishing at the lake and coming up with lyrical gems. It was impossible not to admire their genius. And what about Tom Petty, whom I adored as a teenager? We saw him live, again and again, and yet were blissfully unaware that he, too, displayed that hateful symbol at his concerts, an action that Petty himself would later describe as "downright stupid."

We placed ourselves dead center in hostile territory without even knowing it, embracing those who hated us or, at the very least, who thought less of us than we deserved. Still, what was the alternative? Where were we to go with our budding yearnings and desires for shared community?

The answer to my question came in a single word: Saul. I pictured us traveling the world together, letting our wild hair fly free and rocking out. That is, until he dropped a bomb on me. One morning in homeroom he flashed a woeful glance in my direction, slinking into the seat in front of me without saying a word.

I leaned forward. "What's wrong?"

He shrugged.

"What?" I repeated.

"Nothing."

"Saul's bugging me," I complained to my journal later that day. "He never talks. He's just always giving me these 'Feel sorry for me' looks. Don't ask me why." Even after studying the magazines Mom left on the tank of the toilet (*Cosmopolitan* and *New Woman* especially), it was impossible for me to make out what the other half was thinking. Until I saw them together—Saul and Melissa. Then, I understood.

It was after school one day, on the lawn where the school buses lined up. She sat on his lap, French-kissing him. They came up for air, laughing and holding hands. Melissa was blond and vivacious, with full breasts. Unlike me, she was the chatty type—always thrusting her chest out and tossing her hair at people. She embodied everything I longed to be but was not. She was sexy, fun, outgoing. In a word: white. To my mind, my skinny frame and wild hair were neither cute nor sexy. Not in the way that Melissa was. Certainly not like any of the other flirty white girls the boys always seemed to fall for.

I felt like a fool. What had I been thinking? Saul probably never even noticed me, I realized. Not like that. Still, I got my consolation prize at the end of the school year. To my amazement, Saul and I were both voted "Best Looking" by the graduating class (a compliment I never fully digested at the time), which meant that we had to take a yearbook photo together. It was interesting that two biracial kids would be seen as best looking. We were exotic and unique to 1970s society. Black and white adults alike swooned over biracial babies , as if we were somehow "better" than the norm.

I couldn't wait for picture day. It would be my last chance to make an impression. Maybe Saul wasn't so much into Melissa after all, I convinced myself. On the appointed morning, I subdued my thick hair vigorously, pressing and blow-drying to make it stay flat, stay straight, stay *tame*. Lisa and I had a shorthand for weather alerts whenever an especially foggy or overcast day threatened to undo all our hard work at grooming. We'd yell across the apartment, "It's hair-frizzing weather!" In those cases, the only solution was to pull our hair back tightly into ponytails or tight buns until the moist air passed. Only then would it be safe to let it hang loose again.

Luckily, the sun shone on picture day. Saul and I stood beside each other arranging ourselves into a pose. I smiled as he draped a casual arm across my shoulder. *Cheese.* That photo is out there somewhere, in someone's yearbook, although those middle school journalists weren't much good at fact-checking. Not only is my name misspelled in the caption, but Saul and I both appear mistakenly under the heading "Most Popular," which, as shy as we both were, couldn't have been more wrong.

He was also voted "Most Likely to Become a Famous Guitarist," which was prescient. Of course he was. Saul carted his guitar with him everywhere he went and before long, he would transform himself into "Slash" of the famous band Guns N' Roses, with Steven Adler as his drummer. Years later, I watched from a distance as critics castigated the band's lead singer, Axl Rose, for writing racist lyrics. Saul remained mostly silent about it, focusing on his music and refusing to address the matter publicly. I admired his ability to tune it all out. We were different in that way. While I would grow up to become someone who cared very much what people thought, especially Black people, Saul didn't seem to care much for racial categories at all, much less the judgments of Black folk.

The yearbook photographer collected his equipment and turned to go. I nodded shyly in Saul's direction. "See you around."

"OK. Yeah. See you around."

As the years went by in our apartment on Hollywood Boulevard, I once again pressed my mother for information about my father. Sitting on her bed one afternoon, I nudged the phone in her direction.

"Please? Can we just try?"

"I don't think he lives there anymore" was Mom's careful response.

"Well, maybe he's in trouble and he can't call us. What if he's hurt?"

Mom must have seen the desperation in my eyes. Or maybe she just felt sorry for me. Whatever the reason, she reflected my pain back to me through her own moist gaze, and for a moment, our shared sorrow was enough.

"Did you receive the little red purse?" my father once wrote. I had last heard from him in December 1973, at the age of eight. "There was something inside that was shiny and bright and worth a whole lot . . . like you." The purse was my most prized possession. Fire-engine red, it was patent leather vinyl with pockets and zippers and a long strap, so I could sling it across my shoulder grown-up style. Inside, my father had placed a pile of shiny pennies. "I hope Santa brings you a bunch of goodies because I know you are a very good, good girl," he continued.

My father had been drinking since the age of nine. He wrote that letter at thirty-six years old, five months into his latest attempt at sobriety. "Do you think you could send a picture so that I could carry it with me in my wallet?" It was a request that caused my chest to puff with pride. He also sent a picture of himself: the first I'd ever seen. In it, he crouched beneath a tree with his hound dog, Sadie, holding her in place for the camera. I studied his hair, which was thick and caramel-colored like mine. He looked downward, his gaze directed at the dog.

I wished I could see his face.

After careful consideration, I decided to send him a picture of me in my Brownie uniform, two fingers held up in pledge pose. You look "very pretty and happy," he replied in his next letter, noting that he had also been a Boy Scout:

> I'll bet you get good grades in third grade. You make me very happy when you write to me and I can see that you are a good girl. Bye-bye for now. I love you. XXXXOOOOX Dad

I had lived with those treasured letters and with that long-ago birthday gift for years, believing in them as if they held some sort of magical promise. Yes, my father and I lived apart, but that changed nothing. To my mind, we were still hearts and kisses on the page, now and forever. There had been no marriage between my parents and, therefore, no divorce or tearful goodbyes. For all I knew, he was coming back. Why would I think anything different? No one said anything different. *He was coming back.* To me, the photograph, purse, and letters were proof that my father loved me just as I loved him. I clung to that proof long after I should have—long after it made sense to do so.

Well into adulthood, my father would remain a kind of unspoken prayer—a secret desire I shared with no one. I made the same wish every year over my birthday candles. Squeezing my eyes tight, I would ask God to bring him home, to bring him back to us. There was no question of asking for anything else. He was the one most important thing that was missing. As crazy as it seems to me now, looking back, I didn't stop making that wish until high school. Maybe even college.

It wasn't until later that I would confront him, offering his correspondence back up to him in anger, forcing my father to account for his words. Forcing him to render them true.

"What was he like?"

Mom sighed.

"Oh. He was charming." She smiled. "A free spirit. He really knew how to enjoy life." I stretched out on her bed, willing her to continue. To my surprise, she did, momentarily lost in reverie. It was a rare treat to be privy to Mom's feelings.

"Did I tell you about the time he was in a band?"

I shook my head.

"We had wandered into this little bar on Venice Beach with nothing but a few tables and chairs. Phil took one look around and told the owner, 'You know what you need in here? You need some music. Just a little two-, three-piece band to liven up the place.'" Mom dropped her jaw for dramatic effect. "The next thing you know, your dad had gone to a pawnshop and rustled himself up a saxophone!" She burst into laughter. "Just like that! Then he went out and found a couple of guys from who knows where, and before I knew it, he was in a band! They got paid, too. The guy actually *paid* them to play gigs at this little bar."

I didn't know what made me happier: hearing about my father or that Mom was sharing her feelings with me. Either way, I wanted more.

"He sounds like fun."

She exhaled deeply, studying me. "OK."

She reached into her nightstand for an address book and dialed the number. I held my breath as the line rang. Maybe Mom did too. Once, twice, three times . . . but there was nothing. She hung up, reaching across the bed to offer me a hug. "I'm sorry, Zookie."

"It's OK."

And for a moment, it really *was* OK. For the first time I felt that at least we were in this together, Mom and me.

But that wasn't exactly true.

Unbeknownst to me, Mom had made her own plans. She was now working as a secretary at Legal Aid, and not long after our failed call, she decided to ask one of the investigators to locate my father. Within hours, the detective handed her a slip of paper with an address, like it was nothing. Phillip Zook lived in Camarillo, as it happened, just two hours north of Los Angeles.

After all those years of waiting and wondering, finding him had been almost too easy. Mom shot off a telegram asking my father to get in touch. Back then, if a phone number didn't work, a telegram was the best way to reach someone quickly. Just like that, after nearly a decade of silence, my father was suddenly on the other end of a telephone line.

"What's wrong?" he asked.

Mom was aghast. "What's *wrong*? Nothing is *wrong*. We didn't know where you were. Kristal has wanted to talk to you, or to hear from you, for years. She wrote, but her letters were returned by the post office." There was a long pause as my father processed this. In those days, sending a telegram was expensive and not something ordinary people did unless there was a death in the family or some other extraordinary circumstance.

"You scared me," he replied finally.

Was he actually crying? Mom wondered in disbelief.

"Please, don't ever do that again," my father added before hanging up.

He had revealed nothing. Promised nothing. And since the call changed nothing, Mom thought it best to keep it to herself. What she didn't realize was that in doing so, she left me alone again. Alone to continue speculating and wondering. Alone to go on giving my father the perpetual benefit of the doubt. I stepped into adulthood still genuinely believing that he was innocent in his intentions. He couldn't possibly know where I was and *choose* not to see me. No. He had to be in trouble or lost or somehow incapacitated. Surely, one day, he would find me. My father loved me, of that there was no question in my mind. One day, he would certainly come back for his little girl.

college bound

"Going to McDonald's, if anyone wants anything!"

It was late afternoon, long after the three o'clock dismissal bell had rung in my journalism classroom. But we were on deadline, and as co-editor of the *Sheik Press*, I wouldn't be going home anytime soon. Instead, student reporters and editors hunkered down on deadline days. Hunched over sloping architectural desks, we carved out typeset print with an X-Acto knife. Then, once our sentences were just right, we glued the printed words together, readying the pages for the printing press.

"Bring me back some fries, Baby." Gail Spann, my journalism adviser, flagged me down with dollar bills. She called everyone "Baby," but it still felt special when she said it to me. Gijai, as we called her, was by far the hippest and coolest of my teachers. She wore blue jeans to class and rarely gave lectures. If I recall, her boyfriend played trumpet with Earth, Wind & Fire, which only added to her coolness factor. Most importantly, she created an atmosphere in which we felt ourselves to be adults, with free rein and responsibilities. In her class, I was a journalist first and a high school student second.

"Oh . . . and don't forget?" She tapped my arm. "We still need to fill out those college application forms." I hadn't forgotten. Gijai had promised to read over the essay I'd written for admission to the University of California, Santa Barbara. It was a heartfelt outpouring in which I confessed to not having the perfect grades or the most outstanding SAT scores. Instead, I made a case for myself as someone who was driven and hardworking; someone who had held down jobs—babysitting first, then sales—since the age of twelve. If all went well with my application, I explained, I would become the first person in my family to attend a four-year university.

In addition to Ms. Spann, I had another person at Hollywood High to thank for that: my Advanced Placement English teacher, Mr. Kuhn, who had singled me out some months earlier.

It had been an ordinary day in AP English and we students had been working quietly at our desks when Mr. Kuhn tapped me on the shoulder.

"Kristal. Come with me." I looked up from my assignment, but he was already three feet ahead, expecting me to follow. Gathering my bookbag and sweater, I glanced around the classroom, confused. Why hadn't he called on anyone else? I wondered. Mr. Kuhn moved down the hallway wordlessly, in a crisp, beige linen suit, tapping three or four additional students from other classrooms along the way. I had always liked Mr. Kuhn. He was a straightforward, unsentimental leader who commanded respect. Even in 1981, he walked the halls of Hollywood High as an openly gay man who didn't take mess from nobody. Mr. Kuhn said what he meant and meant what he said.

Once we arrived at our destination, an otherwise empty classroom, he arranged us at a small round table and instructed us to put on the name tag stickers that he'd prepared. "This is Ms. Colby," he said, nodding at an African American woman. "She works in admissions at the University of California, Santa Barbara. Please give her your undivided attention, students."

That was Ms. Colby's cue to begin.

"I know you're probably all familiar with UCLA. But have any of you ever heard of the University of California, Santa Barbara?"

We shook our heads no.

"Well, it's a beautiful campus about a ninety-minute drive from here. It sits on a hill overlooking miles of beaches and the Pacific Ocean." I zeroed in on her professional attire, noting that she wore a dark blue suit and sensible heels. I couldn't remember ever having interacted personally with a Black woman in a suit and heels.

"This makes UCSB an especially good choice for oceanography studies," she continued, ". . . and surfers."

There was muffled laughter at this.

I don't remember anyone else in our small group being Black, which always gave me pause when I thought about it years later. Perhaps there were other students of color—and of various ethnicities and nationalities—but I can't be sure of that either. I only remember it being strange that so few of us had been chosen for this meeting.

Ms. Colby went on, detailing the campus's many attributes and concluded by offering us brochures to take home to our parents. "Does anyone have any questions?"

I raised my hand.

"Yes?" Ms. Colby glanced at my name tag. "Ms. Zook?"

"I want to be a writer. Do you have a major for that?" I was still painfully shy in social situations, but somehow my timidity didn't apply when it came to ambitions and goals. On that front, I had no problem speaking my mind.

Ms. Colby studied me for just a fraction longer than necessary. Years later, I would wonder what she saw. Did she know that I was biracial? Most Black folks were highly attuned to the extra fuzz in my hairline and my distinctly biracial features. Even when they knew I was Black, however, they sometimes hesitated to openly acknowledge me. It was as if they were saying, "*I* know who you are . . . but do *you* know?"

As I looked back at that moment in hindsight, even more questions swirled around in my head. Did Mr. Kuhn know that I was biracial? Had he chosen me for that very reason? And what was Ms. Colby's mandate anyway? Was she sent to Los Angeles specifically to recruit minorities? In 1983, UCSB's diversity was abysmal. Black students represented something like one to two percent of the population. If that was the goal, though, then why weren't there other Black students at the table?

All I knew was that there was no shame in my game. If the university was looking for economically and socially disadvantaged, first-generation college applicants from historically underrepresented racial groups, then, *hello*. I fit the bill.

Ms. Colby smiled. "Do you like to write?"

"Yes."

"What's your favorite book?"

"*I Know Why the Caged Bird Sings.*"

Mom and Dra had passed a worn copy of Maya Angelou's autobiography back and forth to each other first, before later offering it to Lisa and me. We had all read Angelou's story of childhood rape, inhaling it as familiar air. In fact, it was the first book I remember our entire family acknowledging and discussing together. Later, I would understand why it had resonated so powerfully with us.

Ms. Colby nodded. "We have a strong English department. I think you'll like it very much."

My decision wasn't complicated. I needed to get out. Only by leaving Hollywood could I truly begin to create the life I dreamed of. Whether that was in Santa Barbara or Kalamazoo didn't matter. All I knew was that I was ready to color my wings and leave the cocoon.

Just before packing my bags and driving north to an off-campus dormitory, I slipped on a pair of white Keds and summer shorts and hit the town for a last night out. My friend David sped down Olympic Boulevard, steering his Toyota Camry into the gutter lane to bypass traffic. Our destination was the Chocolate Bar, an "underground" club near downtown L.A. that served alcohol all night—or at least until the fire department showed up, which it did frequently.

David was African American and Salvadoran, raised by an immigrant mother and a flock of Salvadoran siblings. Our situations were similar, although in David's case, more extreme. Not only had he never met his Black American father, but his mother and nine siblings refused even to discuss or acknowledge him. Talk about painful secrets. None of that mattered to David and me, though, as we sweated out our worries to the funky bass of the Ohio Players, Parliament, Rose Royce, and Cameo. We may have been fatherless, odd ducks to the rest of the world, but we didn't have to explain ourselves to anybody on the dance floor.

I did not invite my longtime boyfriend. A second-generation Mexican American kid on the football team, he'd recently cheated on me with a white-looking Latina. I was already ambivalent about all men, including him, and his betrayal only gave me further reason to run. Besides, I wasn't nearly ready to examine the reasons why I felt such distrust. The best solution, it seemed to me, was simply to break free and make a fresh start somewhere else. What I didn't know was how challenging that new start and that new environment would be.

In multiracial, international, mixed-up Los Angeles, there had never been any real pressure to know, study, or understand my "blackness." In high school, my friends had been Russian, Filipino, Guatemalan, Salvadoran, African American, Mexican American, and various combinations of the above. Even my geometry teacher wore a sari and a bindi of sandalwood paste on her forehead. Hollywood High was just that kind of place, its halls filled with the sound of every language, from Arabic to Vietnamese.

There, I had been free simply to be. I embraced this freedom on my last night out, letting the music seep into my being, pulsating and reassuring. Its thumping shook my hips hard, fast and slow, as we let loose, dripping with sweat, until morning light. On that late summer night, I was still me: a girl who had never given race much thought at all. But all that was about to change. My life would take a dramatic turn when I arrived in the nearly all-white college town of Isla Vista, California.

activist

My American literature professor burst into the classroom, mumbling hellos beneath a thick gray beard and launching into a complex lecture on semiotics. Elliott Butler-Evans was my favorite professor and unlike anyone else in UCSB's English department. With a specialization in Black feminist theory, he focused on a body of methodologies and philosophies called post-structuralism, a complex field that I was only just beginning to understand.

That day he was teaching Ernest Hemingway's novel *For Whom the Bell Tolls*, but not in any way I had ever seen. The course was called American Fiction after 1917 and had been designed to focus on three authors: Hemingway, F. Scott Fitzgerald, and William Faulkner. Butler-Evans, who had taught at UCSB since 1969, questioned this formula, going to war with his colleagues. Was all American fiction after 1917 white and male? he demanded to know. Against their collective wishes, he inserted classic literary works by Black women novelists into the syllabus: Toni Morrison, Alice Walker, and Toni Cade Bambara. His peers objected vehemently, saying that such a course would be better suited in a separate curriculum, perhaps in a course called Black Women Writers. The contradictions inherent in this logic escaped them.

"Notice the rhetorical dissonance in the phrase."

Butler-Evans paused for us to reflect on the passage he had read aloud— something about masculinity. "Do you hear the textual disruptions?" He jotted phrases on the chalkboard: "textual disruptions" and "rhetorical dissonance." Then he turned to the room of mostly white students. "There's a kind of narrative violence here," he said, "in which readers may find reconfigurations of meaning that Hemingway never intended."

I glanced around at the silent faces, tentatively raising my hand.

"Yes?" Butler-Evans swooped in. Even during his lectures, he often clung to a pack of cigarettes or a jangle of keys. It always gave me the impression that he was just passing through the classroom, on his way to somewhere else.

"Is that what's meant by the 'unconscious' of the text?" I asked.

His eyes widened with excitement. "Precisely." In that moment, Butler-Evans seemed to reassess everything about me. Perhaps that was the moment he decided that I might be worth his time.

"HIRE BLACK WOMEN!" I sat cross-legged in the quad near Storke Tower with a group of women activists, holding one of several placards. We were members of a feminist collective called You Can't Keep a Good Woman Down, borrowing from Alice Walker's collection of short stories. Our members were mostly white. Two of us were Black, one was Pacific Islander, and one, the most radical among us, was Native American, in her forties, and actually not a student at all.

Protesting the lack of women of color faculty was just one of our issues, one that Professor Butler-Evans had encouraged. We also "Took Back the Night" in rallies against rape and sexual violence and marched in solidarity with freedom fighters in Central America. Later, outside the group's activities, I would also take on canvassing and soliciting donations for the Committee for a Sane Nuclear Policy, back when the threat of nuclear annihilation was far more prominent in people's minds than it is today.

Personally, I wanted to write about everything, from patriarchy and poverty at home to covert CIA wars abroad and apartheid in South Africa.

During my first year in college, I was becoming more and more militant about my racial identity and about my identity as a woman. In short, I was radicalized, which to me simply meant in the original Latin sense of the word, that I was determined to get to "the root" of the problems in our society.

Colorism, or intraracial prejudice among Black people, was one of them. I remember reading *In Search of Our Mothers' Gardens* by Alice Walker during that first year and coming upon a sentence that would literally change my life: "What black black women would be interested in . . . is a consciously heightened awareness on the part of light black women that they are capable, often quite consciously, of inflicting pain," she wrote. Never in my life had I heard such a thing. I remember sitting up straighter in bed as I read, allowing this new thought to wash over me.

In 1983, Walker had been the first woman of color ever to win the Pulitzer Prize for fiction for her novel *The Color Purple*. That book, along with Gloria Naylor's *The Women of Brewster Place*, Toni Cade Bambara's *The Salt Eaters*, Toni Morrison's *The Bluest Eye*, and June Jordan's *Living Room*, had revolutionized my thinking. This was contemporary Black feminist literature at its best, and I devoured every word.

And now, Walker spoke to me directly, as a light-skinned Black woman. After reading that sentence, I relived so many scenes in my mind, past responses to my skin color from darker-skinned men and women. I thought about the occasional harsh stares and sideways suspicion that I had sometimes felt. Walker dared me to look more closely at the mutual resentments among us and to examine our shared legacy of pain as well as my own color privilege. In short, she held me accountable while at the same time—and this was the amazing part—inviting me in.

Suddenly, I was part of a conversation that before that moment I had not even known existed. Walker's words changed the way I defined myself. I wasn't "mixed," as Dra and Mom had said all those years. Walker gave me the tools and the language to express my true, authentic self. For the first time in my life, I was not something *outside* of my family. I was part of it. *I was a light-skinned Black woman.*

After the rally was over and our placards were stored away, I came across an acquaintance from Los Angeles on the far side of the quad, a white guy originally from Montana.

"Kristal?"

"Oh, hey, Steve!"

"What are you doing?" I saw that his face was contorted with anger.

"What do you mean?"

"Are you part of this whole thing?"

"Yeah, I wrote an op-ed about it in this week's *Daily Nexus*."

"I can't believe you would be so selfish."

His words floored me. At first, I had no response.

"You're just doing this for yourself!" he spat, eyes ablaze. "So that *you* can get hired one day as a professor!" He shook his head in disgust. "I can't believe that you would be so petty and self-centered! You want it all, but you don't want to work for it!"

Now I was the one who was pissed. *I didn't want to work for it? WTF?*

I'd worked babysitting jobs since I was twelve. At fourteen, I lied on a job application and said I was sixteen so that I could work the four-to-midnight shift at a tourist T-shirt shop on Hollywood Boulevard. I had scrimped and saved every penny to pay for college, and I didn't want to work for it? He went on and on, his body language encroaching into my personal space as he spewed his vitriol. It was the first time I can remember being openly targeted with such anti-Black rage. The incident haunted me for weeks afterward.

At UCSB I wanted desperately to fit in with the white, laid-back surfer culture—that segment of the population known for having the coolest fraternities and keg parties. But I also knew that I was not one of them. To set myself apart, I would sometimes make earnest philosophical arguments over my beer cup. Like saying that my uncle Mervin had in fact been "murdered, in a way," by a system that predetermined his addiction to heroin. At every opportunity, I explained that my African American mother and grandmother raised me, not my white father. Hammering the point home, I insisted that, while my skin may have been light, my innermost self was most definitely Black.

But this stance was complicated by the fact that I still yearned deeply for my own missing white father. What would it mean to have his approval and acceptance, I wondered in some deep part of myself? Could he help me to reconcile these warring parts of myself, the white and the Black?

Soon, I would find out.

Butler-Evans handed my typewritten essays back reeking of nicotine. Typically, I found one or two brief notes in the margins and an A scribbled on the last page. For one, however, he went a step further, calling my analysis "highly sophisticated." Buoyed by his praise, I made plans to enter the campus's W. E. B. Du Bois Writing Contest, an event orchestrated by the Educational Opportunity Program and Office of Student Affirmative Action.

The character of Maureen Peal in Toni Morrison's *The Bluest Eye* is "a self-righteous mulatta who attempts to hurt dark-skinned Black girls by flaunting her imagined superiority," I wrote, revising and correcting my essay again and again with a worn thesaurus. Contest winners would see their work published in a campus journal called *Expressions*. I was determined to be among them.

Squeak from *The Color Purple* is a "feeble character ridiculed by her community," I continued, noting that she lacks the confidence of darker-skinned women characters, such as Shug and Sofia. My thesis was that light-skinned Black women in contemporary literature had devolved over time, moving away from "a myth of preeminence to one of helplessness and unimportance." At the same time, darker-skinned women characters, such as Celie and Sofia, had been empowered during this period of literary history.

Not long afterward, I flew into Butler-Evans's office, thrusting a copy of *Expressions* under his nose. "Have you seen this?"

"Yes," he offered casually. "It came in my mailbox this morning."

Butler-Evans had never been the nurturing type. As a mentor, he was gruff and unsentimental. Still, despite his orneriness, I knew that he liked me. Or maybe I should say that he believed in me, which was quite another thing. Later, he would recommend me as one of the best students he had ever taught, citing my "intense intellectual enthusiasm and curiosity." He also noted that I was "a very modest young woman who is assertive without being aggressive." No matter how ornery he might have been, I knew that he was proud of me.

For the moment, however, he said nothing, continuing to arrange files in a cabinet. My shoulders slumped forward, an indication of my ever-fragile self-esteem. Mom called them "rounded shoulders," reminding me constantly to sit up straight.

"Why are you bothering with that crap?" he offered finally.

"What?"

He sighed, perhaps realizing that his tone was all wrong. "What I mean is that you should be publishing in *professional* journals. Not messing around with that amateur stuff."

There was a compliment in there somewhere.

"But my essay won first place," I protested.

"Yes, but why haven't you applied to graduate schools yet?"

I shrugged.

"Do you have any idea how rare it is for a Black woman to be tenured in the UC system? That's the *real* issue you should be thinking about."

My shoulders slumped further, his comment striking at the heart of my low self-esteem. Angry Montana guy in the quad had been dead wrong. At that point, I had not seen myself as professor material. I had no concept of advanced math and only the shakiest grasp of world history and geography. I knew that I was a good writer, but never in my wildest dreams did I see myself entering the world of advanced scholarship.

Professor Butler-Evans changed that. To his mind, getting a doctorate was my civic duty. He wanted me to represent for the cause. To represent Black people.

Me.

"What you need to do is you need to stop fooling around with these silly contests and apply to graduate school."

I swallowed the emotion in my throat, nodding.

In 1987, the History of Consciousness PhD program at UC Santa Cruz received 210 applications for the coming academic year. Of these, eleven students were chosen for admission. Thanks to Butler-Evans's letter of recommendation, I was one of them. In 1988, I became the first Black woman to enroll in the program in more than a decade. My years at UCSC would be a transformational experience, one that took decades to process. In fact, I don't think I fully grasped how it had shaped me until the summer of 2020, that fateful year when George Floyd was murdered by police and the streets exploded with Black Lives Matter protestors—the same year I wrote publicly about my graduate education for the *New Yorker*, joining thousands of others who confessed their #Black-InTheIvory memories, and arriving, finally, at a kind of belated sense of closure.

light-skinned

Lisa and I always called ourselves biracial, but in fact we were probably something closer to what some have called "quadroons," with about a quarter of African ancestry in our blood. Horace Brent, my maternal grandfather's father, was a white man. He lived in a large house at the top of a shady hill in Tarry, Arkansas, just south of Pine Bluff. The home overlooked a "Brent River," or so the story goes. At the bottom of the hill, down a red clay road, a Black woman named Delphia lived in a rundown wooden shack. She was my great-grandmother.

I once asked Dra about Horace and Delphia while writing a school paper. My grandfather had died before I was born, and Dra didn't know much about his side of the family. But she did remember that Delphia was different from other women in the countryside. Farm women rarely wore makeup, Dra said, but both Delphia and her sister Luveenia were known for wearing "bright bloodred lipstick." I recorded Dra's words on a cassette tape recorder, thrilled to learn more about our heritage. "Also, they were exceptionally tall," she said. "Very tall and very Black. They wore different kind of clothes too. Like some of those island women. You could tell they were from somewhere else."

Horace, my white great-grandfather, had two sons with Delphia, Arthur and Oscar. In my family, we always assumed these children were the products of rape. But unlike most white Southern men of his time, Horace didn't quite fit the mold. For one thing, he publicly claimed his boys, driving them into town with him on Saturdays while he ran errands. What's more, something else added to the mystery of Horace and Delphia.

Our family had always assumed that Horace was married and that he lived with his wife in that big house at the top of the hill. But we were wrong. Many years later, a cousin of ours named Clem Hunter did some research and discovered that, in fact, the woman who lived with him was his sister.

Did Horace love Delphia?

No one knows.

But we do know this.

When he died unexpectedly at a young age, his sister wasted no time in sending a warning down the hill to Delphia. *Be gone before sundown.* My great-grandmother didn't waste a minute speculating about what might happen if she defied her wishes. Delphia hopped right to it, packing her family's meager belongings and setting out to God knows where with her three sons: Arthur, Oscar, and her eldest, Tab, whose father was Caribbean-born. When Delphia also died, not long afterward and at a young age, her sons were sent to live with Delphia's sister, their aunt Luveenia, whose husband wanted nothing to do with Arthur and Oscar, "two little half-white boys," as Dra put it.

So it was that my grandfather, Arthur Sr., was left to make his way alone in the world at age fifteen. He found work on a nearby farm—which, as fate would have it, belonged to a woman named Miss Penny: the grandmother of his future wife, my Dra.

At the intersection where the roads to Moscow and Tarry meet, there are 140 acres of land, possibly still in our family's name and once managed by our cousin Clem. I was never quite clear about where the land came from or how it came to be ours. I know that my grandmother walked that same road as a child, on her way to get fresh buttermilk from Big Ma's farm. She picked plums along the way. Or blueberries and apples; sometimes peaches and pears. Now there is nothing on the surrounding lands but commercial soybean and rice crops for as far as the eye can see. There were once seven brothers to inherit and farm the land, Clem told me. Some of them left for cities such as New Orleans, where they died violent, drug-ridden deaths. Today, the family land sits abandoned, covered with rusty tractors, as if farming were a long-ago lost way of life.

"Girl, you ain't Black! Ha ha! You ain't nothin' but a high-yella gal. Ain't nobody never thought you was Black!" Herschel, a fellow student at UCSB, cackled in his chair, leaning back and slapping his knee. I stared at the freckles splashed across his light-skinned nose, which, truth be told, was only a damn shade darker than my own. I was living with my boyfriend, Jaime, in an off-campus apartment. Herschel was Jaime's friend and former roommate.

"Come on, now. *Girl.* Tell the truth. What are you doing with this guy?" He nodded across the room at Jaime, who was white with platinum-blond hair.

"Fuck you." Jaime flipped burgers in the kitchen, unfazed.

I had met Jaime as a sophomore and liked that he was a political activist. I also liked that Bob Marley's "Is This Love" blared from his stereo on weekends and that he worked his way through college as a pastry chef, speaking broken Spanish in dormitory kitchens. He led marches to protest apartheid in South Africa and had even gone to jail for his beliefs. Perhaps more importantly, he came from a large and loving family, with three adopted siblings of color. None of these things made him Black, of course, but for me, they did put him somewhere outside the typical category of whiteness. If I was searching the eyes of men for my own reflection, Jaime was the closest I had come yet.

An added bonus was his parents, whom I adored. Practicing psychologists, they represented the first healthy marriage I'd ever seen up close. After four decades together, they still confided in and respected one another, walking on the beach and holding hands as part of their morning ritual. For a time, Jaime and I even camped out in their converted garage bedroom. Watching them interact gave me a blueprint I'd never had as a child. For the first time in my life, I understood what a truly loving partnership was supposed to look like.

"Girl!" Herschel cackled again. "You better listen to me. *Listen to me.* I'm telling you right now. You better go and get yourself a *Black* man!"

I laughed too, pretending his words had no effect on me. But that was a lie. Herschel's jabs and my own insecurities had taken a toll in ways that I could never fully explain to anyone, not even to Jaime. For me, being biracial made even the most inconsequential choices seem monumental. Every alliance, every smile or nod, seemed to represent the affirmation or rejection of an entire heritage. Friendships and lovers were up for scrutiny by the collective, too, as I had recently learned.

My friend Helen, a Chinese American not-yet-out lesbian from San Francisco, talked Blackish and showed up regularly at our Black Student Union meetings. For whatever reason, she identified with African American culture and apparently felt more at home in those circles, with us, than in other spaces on campus. Still, a small group of BSU members decided to vote her out of the union after a special meeting. A few even implied that my friendship with her made me somehow suspect as well. Somehow less authentically Black.

Having light skin meant that I was guilty until proven innocent. Some assumed, without even knowing me, that I saw myself as "better than" darker-skinned Black folks. Their suspicion was understandable. It didn't come from nowhere. In fact, there was a long and painful history behind such unspoken resentments. A history of passing, privilege, and paper bag tests. Our identities were fraught on all sides. Now, to choose a white partner over a Black one seemed only to add to my original sin. "What next?" a Black girlfriend asked me one day, only half-joking. "White babies?"

Jaime and I were an interracial couple at a time when America had not yet seen a single television commercial or printed advertisement featuring couples of different races or mixed-race families. It seems hard to imagine today, but that kind of cultural norm in marketing would not become prevalent until *decades* later. If I had felt alone and invisible before, as a biracial woman, then being with Jaime only made me doubly so. I was a nearly white woman with a white boyfriend. There wasn't a Black person on the street who would give me "the nod" now.

My insecurities about race, coupled with my deep-rooted and still mostly unconscious fears about men, were paralyzing. Together, they stopped me from diving headlong into the relationship. I withheld pieces of myself. I put up armor. It made no sense. But then, fear rarely does.

I dreamed that there was a massive fundraiser and every single Black person on campus was asked to contribute original sewing. I was embarrassed and unsure of myself as I approached the crowd. But then someone handed me a piece of cloth and a sewing kit and told me I could contribute from anywhere I felt comfortable. "Wherever you like," they said. I accepted the items gratefully, deciding that I would go wherever I needed to go to do my part.

My high school journalism teacher, Gijai Spann, wrote me from time to time, cheering me on. "I am very proud of you!" she said upon hearing about the W. E. B. Du Bois contest. "Read *Black Voices*, especially 'The Origin and Growth of Afro-American Literature' by John Henrik Clarke! And keep up the great work!" Her encouragement meant the world to me. And yet, I longed for someone who could help me navigate the treacherous waters of mixed-race identity. The only other biracial Black girl I knew on campus was from South Central Los Angeles, wore her hair in cornrows, and looked down at me for "talking white."

There was no one.

For years, I wrestled with my outsider-insider identity in any number of settings. In fact, it wasn't so long ago that I caught a cab from Newark's international airport late one night. Flash forward to 2006, long after my college years. I was a working journalist on my way home to a one-bedroom rental at 145th Street and Edgecombe Avenue in Harlem. The taxi was driven by a Colombian woman whose teenage daughter sat beside her in the passenger seat. I had scarcely given the address, finishing with the word "Harlem," when I overheard her speaking to her daughter in Spanish.

"Si hubiera sido Negra no la hubiera llevado."

If I had been Black, she said, she never would have picked me up. I was amazed. In the flash of an instant, she had come to the conclusion, one, that I wasn't Black, and, two, that I didn't speak Spanish.

"Perdone. ¿Que ha dicho?" I asked her to clarify. My Spanish caught her off guard, I think, but she plunged forward anyway. Without missing a beat, she explained that Black people in Harlem were all the same. They either robbed you or left you with an unpaid bill. I said nothing, measuring my rage.

Part of me had zero interest in engaging. It was after midnight and I was exhausted from my travels. All I wanted was a hot shower and my warm bed. Another part of me, however, knew that I had no choice. Being biracial was sometimes like being the only one in the room able to turn a diamond and to see, truly, all the different colors visible from different angles.

We rode in silence for a while until she pulled up to my apartment building and clicked the meter. I handed her just enough cash to pay the bill, and not a dime more. "Now you can tell your friends that you picked up a Black person and absolutely nothing happened," I said. Her gaping mouth was the last thing I saw in the rearview mirror as I slammed the door and walked away.

For me, the fact of being locked outside the safety of any one home would eventually become a kind of resting place in itself. Yes, I was alone. Outside. But at least there I had the best view of the stars. Still, as a young person in college, I wasn't anywhere close to that kind of self-knowledge. I wouldn't get there for many years to come.

"I had a nightmare last night," I confessed to Jaime. We were wrapping up our Thursday evening weekly ritual of home-cooked food, cheap wine, and *The Cosby Show*. As a finale, we'd fired up the small, above-ground Jacuzzi in the backyard of his parents' home and slid in for a whirlpool massage. Jaime knew how much I believed in dreams. Dra raised me to pay attention to their messages. If I dreamed of a frog, she would look it up in a special dream dictionary and read the definition to me over the phone.

I hesitated before sharing this one, though.

"Tell me."

I inhaled deeply, knowing that sharing the dream would be the equivalent of saying goodbye.

"I was loading a suitcase onto a bus that I was supposed to take with you, but at the last minute, I got off and got on a different bus that was driven by a Black woman. I asked her to follow you, but she said she couldn't."

Tears streamed down my face.

"It's OK." Jaime took me into his arms. "It's going to be OK." But it wasn't.

After more than two years together, I was beginning to realize that I had a long and painful road ahead and that Jaime would not be able to travel it with me.

I continued to study my dreams, tracking them in my journal and hoping for further insights. The more I listened, the more furiously they came, offering me constant clues and a gateway to understanding. In one, a shy ghost child climbed a long, spiral staircase ascending into the clouds. It bothered me that I could see only parts of her body—an arm, a floating scarf around an invisible neck. "Can you show me more?" I asked. "Why?" She lashed out. "Why does it matter what I look like?"

Even more disturbing were what I called my "bathroom dreams"— recurrent nightmares in which I was constantly trying to outrun men who would do me harm. The bathroom dreams always ended the same way: with me taking refuge in one bathroom or another. It didn't matter where or what kind. They were public and private, glamorous and dingy. I dreamed of everything from outhouses on dirt roads to gold-plated powder rooms in luxury hotels. There were bathrooms of every kind, all night, every night. The dreams battered my psyche, as though my brain were trying to fit together a puzzle with missing pieces.

As an adult, I've often been too demanding, the textbook definition of a perfectionist. At times, I don't leave enough room in my heart for the fact that people are human and make mistakes and have failings. My judgments are especially harsh when it comes to myself. I find it incredibly difficult to be wrong. Screwing up, even in small ways, is enough to send me reeling, hiding under my covers with shame.

One morning, after I had drunk too much beer, and said and done things I regretted, I marched myself into the university counseling center and asked for an urgent walk-in appointment. The university offered ten free therapy sessions, I was told. I scheduled them all, on the spot, and began showing up regularly to talk to a graduate psychology student in training.

On the day of my final, tenth session, the student therapist asked if there was anything else that I wanted to talk about. Incredibly, I hadn't mentioned the bathroom dreams to her, and so, in the closing minutes of that final hour, I decided that it was worth a try.

"Well . . . I've been having these nightmares. . . ."

"Oh? What are they about?"

"I don't know. . . ." I hesitated. "They're strange. I'm always running away from men who want to hurt me."

She thought for a moment, shifting in her seat. "Hurt you how?"

"Rape me, I guess."

She glanced at her watch. I had sprung this information on her with less than ten minutes on the clock. She exhaled.

"Well . . . Have you ever been raped?"

"No. Of course not." I answered too quickly. Automatically.

But then, just as I spoke, a vivid image flashed before my mind's eye for the first time. As a memory, it was undeniable. Sharp. Clear. I saw green shag carpet. I saw the little girl version of myself, pressing my knees into my chest, backed against a wall on the Noches' bedroom floor in my long, flannel nightgown. In that instant, I remembered skooching my body backward, trying to get away, and the electrical shocks caused by the friction of my nightgown against the carpet.

"I mean . . . well . . ." I backtracked. "I don't think so."

The therapist pressed her lips together. Was she as detached as she seemed to be?

"Dreams can offer clues to our feelings," she offered. "Why don't you try writing yours down in a notebook? That sometimes helps."

"OK." I gathered my book bag, preparing to leave.

"Kristal, if you need more sessions . . ."

I forced a smile. "No. I'm OK. Bye." Turning, I escaped before she could see my tears.

taking a chance

From my off-campus apartment in Santa Barbara, I picked up the phone and dialed 411, once again on a renewed quest to find my father. "City and state?" The operator's voice was strangely computer-like in an era when almost no one had computers.

"Phoenix, Arizona."

"Go ahead."

"Do you have a number for Phillip Zook?"

Although I probably could not have expressed it at the time, I sensed that something profound was missing in my life. It was a muddled, murky feeling. Like my glasses were perpetually smudged and I just couldn't quite see clearly. I hadn't pieced it together then, but eventually I would realize that the timing of my father's last letters coincided roughly with my assault by Fernando Noche, as luck would have it. My father had never been physically present, but because of his letters I must have believed that he would eventually come back. After Fernando Noche my child's mind must have wondered, *Was my father mad at me for what happened? Had I done something wrong to make him go away . . . again?* I sensed that no one could cure whatever it was that ailed me. I could either move forward with my life or stay exactly where I was. It was my choice.

"Please hold." The operator checked the directory.

"There is no listing for a Phillip Zook in Phoenix, Arizona."

I bowed my head, defeated. Still, some part of me wasn't ready to give up.

During college I sometimes trekked home to our apartment on Hollywood Boulevard, although things weren't quite as I would have liked there. For one thing, Mom had married a Frenchman while I was away—a surly man who wasn't particularly kind. What's more, Mom's new husband didn't speak much English and seemed to have zero interest in getting to know me. I suspected he was after a green card. In the end, my suspicions were warranted. He would turn out to be an "asshole," as my mother later confessed.

But at the time, she remained as emotionally aloof as ever. Quick to criticize, as she herself acknowledged, and slow to affirm. Sometimes I felt that I couldn't catch a break in our interactions; even the most benign conversation was fraught with tension. I was on high alert with her, never knowing when she might make a derisive comment about my makeup or hair or something I said. The divide between us only grew wider during my college years.

On one visit home she overheard me belting out the lyrics to Bob Marley's "Babylon System." "Yeah, we've been trodding on the winepress much too long. . . . Rebel! Rebel!" I sang out.

My mother looked aghast, as though personally offended. She stopped whatever she was doing and stared at me. "You ain't been trodding on no winepress!" she snapped. I suppose in her view I wasn't oppressed. It was certainly true that I didn't grow up in that kind of abject poverty. Nor had I ever been persecuted for the color of my skin. But couldn't Mom just let me sing the song? Couldn't some small part of it be mine to claim? If I was looking for a shoulder to lean on as I muddled through the conflicted waters of race loyalty and identity, it was clear that I wasn't going to find it on her.

Usually, I got home in time to eat, change clothes, and head out to the Palladium on Sunset Boulevard for a night of dancing. A friend worked security and let me slip into the roped-off VIP section, where I would spend the evening flirting with Tone Loc or perhaps one of the Tony! Toni! Toné!s. I had this goal in mind as I approached the city of Camarillo, just south of Santa Barbara.

It was a familiar marker. I'd driven past it on countless occasions over the years, coming to and from college. But somehow, on this particular afternoon, something about it tugged at my memory. *What was it that Mom had said about my father?* I thought. *Something about a hospital in Camarillo?*

I'd passed the exit so many times before and never once had I thought to stop. Why today? I had no idea. Only that something told me to get out. *Now.* Before I knew what was happening, I'd swerved my secondhand Chevy Chevette toward the off-ramp and pulled into a service station. Parking next to a phone booth, I flipped open the directory to the white pages and scanned for Zooks. To my amazement, there were several. My heart leapt. It wasn't a common name. Surely, one of these people must know something about my father.

I considered going down the list and calling them all but quickly decided against that idea. If I was going to find my father today, I was determined that it should happen in person. I scanned the list again. Only one of the listings—someone named Eric Zook—gave an actual address. That made my decision easy. There was only one possibility for me that day, only one person that I was meant to see. I bought a city map from the gas station attendant and set out for a street called Calle Bella Vista.

The sun had nearly sunk into the horizon when I knocked on the apartment door. A handsome man answered, possibly in his late twenties. Tall and slender like me, he had thick caramel-colored hair.

"Sorry to bother you." I tried not to let my shoulders slump forward. "My name is Kristal and I'm looking for a Phillip Zook?"

I could hear clanking plates and utensils in the background. Someone cooking dinner. Suddenly, my words sounded ridiculous even to me. Why did I care so much about a father I'd never known? Why couldn't I just let it go? Just as I was wishing I had never come, a slight smile crept across the stranger's face.

"Hi. I think you must be . . . my sister."

"What?"

"Yeah. That's my dad. Phil Zook."

I felt woozy. As if I'd just won the lottery.

I had a brother? And he knew my father?

Eric ushered me into the living room. "Trish, can you come out here for a sec?" A woman appeared from the kitchen, and he introduced her as his fiancée. They had guests that evening, who also appeared then: a young couple with a baby. Eric explained who I was to everyone in a scene that was both profoundly awkward and surreal. Eric and Trish had questions, too. How did I find them? And where was my mother? Did she know I was here? And did I want anything to eat or drink? In a flash, my life was transformed. Suddenly, these people who lived off a highway I had traveled for years were my family?

"I only recently found our dad myself," Eric confided. *Our dad.* The words sounded so foreign. And what did he mean that he had "found" him? Eric explained that he had an older brother and a younger sister and that our father, still doing drugs and drinking in those days, had left them all as children, just before he went to live on Venice Beach.

At twenty-one, Eric had been living in San Francisco with his mother and siblings when he decided to hitchhike to Camarillo to try to find our father. It wasn't hard. He had been right there all along, living with his second wife and their two children, our youngest siblings. "I even lived with them for a while," Eric said, a flash of pride lighting his face. "We worked together, doing landscaping. I'm a gardener too. Like Dad."

My jaw dropped. Did he mean to tell me that my father and brother had been right here, just two hours north of Los Angeles, all these years? I pushed down the lump in my throat, forcing myself to ask the question.

"When?"

"Let's see . . . that would have been about 1983."

The year I graduated from high school. The same year I made my way up the coast to attend college at UC Santa Barbara. I had passed right by them. My father and brother had been right here, becoming reacquainted, working side by side together in the California sunshine. Without me.

"Where is he now?" I asked.

Eric's face fell. He hesitated, searching for the words to explain something I could see that he himself still didn't understand. "They left. Moved to Vashon. It's a small island in Washington State. I have his new address if you want it."

The mood shifted. At that moment, something in my brother shut down. I watched as he relived his own pain, suddenly realizing that we both had scars. What heartache he must have felt. After having bravely sought out our father—traveling alone across the state to find him and having the emotional fortitude to forgive him—Eric had woken up one morning to find himself left behind, once again.

He handed me one of his landscaping business cards, jotting our father's phone number and address on the other side. I gave him my phone number as well. As I stood to leave, I felt my legs weaken. Still, I remained cool on the outside. Holding it together emotionally, just as Mom and Dra had taught me. Eric and I let out small, subdued chuckles as we embraced and said our goodbyes.

"Keep in touch," he offered.

"Yeah. You, too."

Back in the car, I stared at the card he had given me. A chill went through my bones, and for a moment I shivered so hard that I had to turn on the heater despite the tepid temperature. The reunion I'd longed for my entire life was finally here. I'd found my father.

His reply to my letter came in an envelope postmarked from Vashon. The stationery was light blue, with a logo for "The Gardener" printed across the top. I held my breath as I prepared to read the words I had waited to hear my entire life:

> Kristal, I want you to know that I never stopped thinking about you. I had a lot of troubles for a lot of years and I wouldn't have made anybody a good father. Alcoholism and drug addiction led me down many dark paths and through the gates of insanity. I am sure that it was God's will that you didn't know me then. I always thought that when the time was right, we could make a beginning. . . . Things have not been easy, but I have made progress, thanks to God.

My father told me that he had been "thrilled" to receive my letter. "It is amazing how things can change overnight," he wrote. "I now have another daughter."

But did he?

dad

"You're going to love Santa Cruz," my father wrote as I prepared for my first semester of graduate school at UCSC. "I visited the campus years ago and it was a place of peace and tranquility. I especially liked the library with the big windows full of hundred-year-old trees." My father's letters always contained some commentary on nature: a view of foliage from his window, changing seasons, weather conditions. His home on Vashon Island was quiet, with "only birds and an occasional rooster to shatter the silence." There were "bracken ferns and century-old pines and a hill covered with runaway blackberries and sweet peas." Later, he would add photos to his messages: a cluster of fall crocuses, a hybrid red rose. His appreciation for the natural world was akin to a spiritual practice. We had that in common.

I could see, too, that he genuinely wanted to reconnect. We were "beginning again," as he put it. "We should get together one of these days. Do you ever plan on a visit?" He offered to pay for airfare so that I could travel to Vashon for my birthday. "I hope I am not being push and shove. I would really like you to come visit."

I should have been overjoyed. My lifelong dream had come true. *My father was back.* But something in me hesitated. Somehow, a deeply protective instinct had taken over, setting in motion a conflicting agenda in which I both hungered for a relationship with my father and kept him at arm's length. Instead of enjoying the milestone moments in our budding relationship, part of me feigned indifference, taking on my mother's cool air. As long as I could control the unfolding of events, setting strict emotional limits and boundaries, I believed that he couldn't hurt me again.

I would be in the driver's seat now.

As a result, my own letters were alternately affectionate and withdrawn. At times, I'd take a chance and reveal my innermost thoughts, yearning for a similar flood of sentimentality from his side. When that failed, I would shut down again, raising protective walls. Mostly, I crowded my letters with questions, desperate to understand why he had abandoned me in the first place. *When was the last time you saw me? How did you feel about it? Why did you leave?*

His answers came haltingly, if at all.

I don't remember much about those days because I was always drugged or drunk. I tried to make a life with your mom and you, but the drugs and booze always got in the way—so I ran away. I was always afraid, and I always ran. . . . I think about you often and wonder what is going on. I guess I am afraid that I have let you down and if we start over, I will let you down again. I know I feel guilty for not being a better father for you. Anyway, I am here now, and I am sober and halfway sane. I love you. I have tried to write and torn up about five letters. I guess I'll just go ahead and mail this.

I could feel his sincerity on the page, and yet, he told me none of the things that the little girl in me needed to hear. Like how much he had missed me all these years. Had he been happy to see me at Venice Beach in my new velvet dress? And most of all, why didn't he try to find me once he got sober? The child in me longed to embrace her long-lost father, but the grown-up woman just couldn't allow it. In his letters, I read a stubborn refusal to acknowledge the still-raw, open nature of my wounds. He was simply unable or unwilling to reassure me or to smooth over all the jagged years of pain. Instead, he merely reiterated what I already knew:

that he was a drug addict and alcoholic who didn't remember much about the bad old days.

With Michele, his current wife, my father had two children: Jennifer, who was fourteen, and Dominic, ten. With the help of a twelve-steps program, he had been sober and employed for fifteen years. It wasn't lost on me that those kids had come home to a father every day, for all the days of their life. Something about that simple fact got under my skin too. To add insult to injury, my father blithely informed me that he shared my letters with his family.

"We love to hear from you," he wrote.

We?

"Jennifer is looking at colleges and taking placement tests. She really is impressed with you. She looks up to you like a big sister that she would like to know better." When I refused the bait, he dug in again. "Jennifer would like to correspond with you. Your letter about the apartment and the writer you are really moved her. You sound like everything she wants to be. She is editor of the high school newspaper."

When I confided that I had been going through bouts of crying and depression, my father informed me that "Jennifer is going through some of the things that you describe. She has not been very happy. She has chosen film this year and has made some pretty amazing films. I think you and she need to communicate."

Need to communicate?

Couldn't he see that this was *my* time? My chance? I'd waited long enough. Why did I now have to share my long-lost father with *them*?

Occasionally, I made offhand complaints to friends about his "*Brady Bunch*–perfect family." Those white kids were nothing like Lisa and me, I'd say bitterly. They grew up in a nice, stable home with Mom and Dad, while we were here, barely hanging on. What's more, I also knew that if it came right down to it, my father would choose his new family over me again, just as he'd done before. I'd yearned for his presence all these years, but now my guard was up. There was no way I would take it down. Not even for him.

In a tiny cabin in the Santa Cruz Mountains, I sprawled out across my futon, which was wedged between a Staples desk and a microwave.

"Hi, Dra."

"Oh, hi, sweetheart." My grandmother always answered the phone with those exact same three words. I called every Sunday, leaning on her for support.

"How are your classes going?"

"Alright. Hard. I've been studying all weekend but . . ." I glanced out the window, tears welling. "I don't know."

The History of Consciousness program at UC Santa Cruz was famous in scholarly circles for its thick post-structuralist theory and obscure academic jargon. Seminars were heavy with talk of concepts such as "humanistic closure," "hermeneutics," "hegemony," and "Manichaean dichotomies." In one class, someone actually referred to, and I quote, "a genealogy of the metonymic transformation and the resulting allegory." To say that I felt out of place was the understatement of the year.

My study method had been to underline entire sections of books, circling unfamiliar phrases and recording my struggling interpretations in the margins. The process was grueling. I had to stop constantly to look up words in the dictionary: callow, monsoon, stalwart, dhoti, and monticule. Often, six or seven hours had passed since I'd eaten. I was well behind my peers academically, and no matter how much I read or took notes, I could never seem to catch up. I didn't belong here, I decided. I was not an intellectual.

I'd read somewhere that only half of those who start doctoral programs finish. To meet the challenge, I laid down some ground rules for myself early on: *Break it into pieces. Write daily. Get a computer. Don't isolate yourself.* My last rule proved to be the most difficult of all. I had holed up in a tiny studio cabin in Felton, a working-class mountain community that was a twenty-minute drive from campus. This was no college town. In fact, there were rumors of a Ku Klux Klan chapter in the area. Once, when an African American girlfriend came to visit me, a stranger spit on her Afro as we exited the local CVS.

I related this to Dra now, on the phone, along with a few other incidents. Like the time I was out jogging in an old "Portugal" T-shirt and a neighbor doing yard work eyed me suspiciously, narrowing his eyes. I was wearing long cornrow braids then, which must have added to his confusion. He gestured at my shirt. "So, is that where you're from then?"

Dra had a simple solution: "Forget about people who just want to drag you down."

"Yeah." I played with my braids, not exactly sure how to do that.

She shifted gears. "Are you eating enough?"

I had Top Ramen in my cupboards, mostly. "Yes."

"Well, let me send you a hundred dollars, at least, for some new underwear and bras." Having fresh lingerie at the start of each school year had always been something of an obsession for Dra.

"Are you sure?" No one in our family understood how Dra managed to stash away so much cash on a housekeeper's wages. She was like Oseola McCarty, the washerwoman who famously donated her life savings of $150,000 for needy students at the University of Southern Mississippi. Once, Dra wired $10,000 to a relative hoping to escape an abusive husband. "Take those kids and leave the state," she told her. "And this is not a loan," she added. "I don't want you out there struggling to pay me back."

"I'm very sure." Dra brightened her voice for emphasis. "It would make me happy to help, and I can afford it. You're working so hard on your studies. I'm just so proud of you."

Dra was my lifeboat in every way, especially during those lonely college years. I suspect, looking back, that her attentiveness to me as a working student was partly rooted in regret. While she nurtured me like a mother hen throughout my long decade of higher education, she had done nothing of the kind for my mother, who briefly tried to attend college at age seventeen before giving up for lack of funds. It was a defining moment in their relationship, and one that explained so much about the resentful, codependent dynamic between Mom and Dra.

After my grandfather died of colon cancer, Mom, who was then seventeen, received a social security payout in death benefits. She used the money to enroll at the Chicago College of Commerce for court reporting, where she excelled in her studies. My mother has always had a sharp intellect. She taught me to figure things out on my own; to look up words I didn't know in the dictionary; to revise my sentences until they were correct. To me, she had the mind of a natural-born editor, writer, or perhaps a lawyer. She instilled in me a love of words, beginning when she was pregnant and she checked out library books on a weekly basis to read to me in the womb.

Once the social security benefit money expired, however, Dra insisted that Mom get a job. She tried to attend night school, after work, but the late hours and the long commute on public transportation were too much. Mom dropped out and never set foot in a college classroom again. She remained bitter about this her entire life, often pointing out that my grandmother continued to gamble money away that might have paid for her tuition. One of her teachers had even come to the house personally, to beg Dra to let my mother come back to school.

Instead, a rift grew and spread between them, which never healed. Mom left her studies and continued working. A few years later, she was pregnant with me.

We chatted a while longer, with Dra eventually returning to a familiar theme. "Now, listen. The next time you come home, I want to give you the key to my lockbox." She kept thousands of dollars in cash inside a safe-deposit box at a Santa Monica bank.

"OK. Why?"

She sighed. "It's just something I want to do. Remember now. You and me will be the only ones with a key, you hear?"

"Yes."

As the years went on, it became clear to all of us that Dra trusted fewer and fewer people. Her beliefs were contorting with age and cementing themselves into permanence. Often, she insisted that family members, and even some of our dearest friends, were under voodoo spells and out to get us. We would realize only later that these suspicions and delusions had first taken shape many years earlier.

In the 1970s, for example, after dating a man from Calvary Baptist Church, Dra became obsessed with random dirt outside our front door. She examined it closely, believing it to be a concoction laid down by her ex-lover to harm our family. In addition to burning candles nonstop, she invested in cleansing incense. Lisa and I were made to stand naked over pots of smoke to block evil forces from entering our bodies on a regular basis.

As a young person, I didn't particularly question these beliefs. There *were* evil forces out there, after all, weren't there? All of us believed in supernatural powers, and it certainly *was* possible that someone had put a generational curse on our family, as Dra believed, going all the way back to the family of Horace Brent, my white great-grandfather in Arkansas. Dra believed that the curse was to make future generations of her children fatherless. And lo and behold, they were. This was true for Lisa and me, and for our four cousins. In fact, not one of Dra's six grandchildren grew up with a father. For us, the idea of a curse didn't seem so far-fetched.

In retrospect, though, it became clear that my grandmother had simply been hurt too deeply, perhaps irreparably, over the course of a lifetime. Something, or a multitude of somethings, had left her unable to trust. Dra's own mother died when she was two, and she once told me that her mother's mother had also died inexplicably young, leaving behind eight children. Dra struggled to understand this pattern of loss, yearning for something she had never had.

Although she was raised by a kind and loving stepmother, I could tell that she longed for her birth mother in the same way that I longed for my absent father. Dra once described her mother, Fanny, to me, saying that she was "tiny, small, and fierce. Light into you in a minute." I remember she chuckled a little at this, adding, "Little bit like me."

Her mother's father, Big Pa, was a proud, dark-skinned man, she said. Like Delphia, my great-grandmother on the other side of the family, Big Pa was from one of the Caribbean islands, although Dra wasn't sure which one. "He wasn't your average run-of-the-mill farmer, I know that much," she said. "He had his own land and didn't have to work for white people. His children grew up working on *his* land." His wife, Big Ma, was classy too, Dra said, a home economics teacher in a local school who taught girls how to make loaves of bread and keep house. I could hear the pride in her voice when she talked about the upright and proud people she had come from.

I sighed now, resigned to the fact that she wanted no one but me to have that key to her lockbox. It was tragic, really. She believed the world was out to get her.

"Let me pray with you before we hang up."

"OK."

Dra didn't just pray over the phone. She *prayed*.

"Heavenly Father." She began slowly, in subdued tones, working her way into more fierce exaltation. "I come to you today with my granddaughter, Kristal. And oh, Heavenly Father . . ." Gradually, her voice began its ascent. "I'm *asking* you to surround her today with your protection, and to wash her in the blood of Jesus Christ, our Lord and Savior. I come to you today, oh Lord, because you said I could."

I nodded, my skin tingling.

"And because you said you would listen when I called your name. And, oh Lord, I'm asking these things today in the name of the Father, and the Son, and the Holy Spirit. We thank you for the blessings that you have bestowed upon us and that you continue to bestow. Amen."

"Amen."

There was something calming in her supplications. No matter what demons I faced, I knew that Dra would be right there by my side, raising her sword against them. Her support comforted me in ways that I didn't yet fully appreciate. I was still under the illusion that I was a strong, independent Black woman who didn't need anyone. But one thing was true: I needed my Dra.

"Well, sweetheart . . . I don't want to run up your phone bill." Just as she began our calls with the same few words, she also ended them, each time, with this exact same sentence. Even many years later, when cell phones and unlimited minutes were ubiquitous, she would repeat this closing line like clockwork.

"I miss you, Dra." My eyes grew moist.

"I miss you too, sweetheart. Grandmommy loves you, you hear?"

"Yes. I love you, too."

My father's letters hovered somewhere between poetry and the ravings of someone who had taken too many psychedelic trips. I enjoyed reading his wacky, earnest musings. Like when he wrote, "I've been reflecting on ancient theory concerning invisible worlds, astrology, astronomy, and the understanding of fear." We talked about everything in our letters. Like when I discovered my own innate love of gardening, he gave me tips, explaining how to get rid of pests. For aphids, he recommended a spray mixture of onion, garlic, and liquid detergent. For snails, beer in a pie dish with salt worked, but you shouldn't put it too close to roots, he warned. For gophers, he offered up a castor oil recipe.

But we never got to the deeper hurts.

He seemed not to understand the power of what he had taught me as a girl: that I was not worth coming back for. That I was not worth defending or protecting. The truth was, I had never recovered from this blow. We should have been saying these things aloud, forcing them into daylight. Instead, we spun our wheels politely, our relationship stunted by all that remained unspoken. At some point, I gave up and simply stopped writing. For several years, his name remained absent even from my journals.

Lisa and I, too, drifted apart—a gradual rift that had begun in high school and became more pronounced during my college years. We spoke by phone and visited when I was home, but with an unspoken longing wedged between us. I made a point to call her every year on the anniversary of her father's death, although I wasn't sure it did much good. I couldn't heal her sadness any more than she could heal mine.

abd

There were seven incoming students in the History of Consciousness program at UC Santa Cruz that year: five white men and women, me, and a Chicano from Nogales, Arizona, named Raúl. One afternoon, the conversation in our first-year seminar turned to race. Our professors, Donna Haraway and Jim Clifford, were two of the most formidable minds I had ever met. The conversation was stimulating, as I recall. Something about how racial meaning is socially constructed, rather than strictly biological. I was only just beginning to wrap my head around post-structuralist theory, and the concepts were still fresh and new.

It soon became apparent, however, that a young woman in our cohort was becoming agitated. I'll call her Mary. She shifted in her seat as though biting her tongue. Finally, she blurted, "It's just that I'm Italian American and . . . I get really tan in the summer." She paused, searching the room. No one had a clue what she was getting at. Raúl and I exchanged confused looks, waiting for her to complete her thought.

"I mean, I get even darker than *her*," she said, crooking her chin in my direction. And then she hit me with it. "So . . . I don't understand. Why does *she* get to be Black?" I wish I could say that someone had a good response to what Mary had said. If they did, I don't recall. I only remember the silence.

I was isolated in a program in which not a single student or faculty member looked like me, or my mother, or my grandmother. All around me were hippie-like surfer students—white kids who found it perfectly acceptable to walk the woodsy paths barefoot on a warm day, or to wear their straight hair in clumped mats that I suppose they thought emulated dreadlocks. For so many of them, college was an inevitable part of growing up. They treated the privilege with a certain casualness that I, as a first-generation student of color, did not share.

Not long afterward, I sat with a small group of Black women—colleagues and students from various departments around campus—at an informal gathering. The conversation had been light and chatty until someone made the following declaration: "I can't stand these light-skinned women."

I glanced around the room, confused.

Did she mean me?

Had to. I was the only one.

"You know the kind . . ." The woman spoke in general terms. "They suddenly come into consciousness and then have the nerve to preach to the rest of us."

I raced through recent events in my mind, horrified. *Had I done that? Had I preached to her*? I couldn't imagine it was true. But then I became enraged. If it was true, then why hadn't she just talked to me? *Weren't we friends*?

"Yeah, but we're all Black," someone ventured, slicing the silence.

One of my mentors jumped in next, a professor who'd taken me under her wing. Surely, she'd set the conversation right. But, to my dismay, she did nothing of the kind. Instead, she surveyed our small cluster and spoke three simple words that broke me in half:

"Well. *Sort of.*"

All my adult life I had fought to be loyal to the cause. I was a race woman through and through. I would not pass for white because I knew where I came from. "I'm biracial but I was raised by Black women," I would explain to anyone who needed to know. It was my way of defining who I could, and could not, be. I could not be white because I had never known a single white mother, sister, aunt, grandmother, or cousin. I could not be white because I had never had white arms wrap themselves around me and cradle me to sleep. I could not be white because white people hurt and degraded my family every day. I could not be white. How I looked had nothing to do it.

And yet, I came to realize that how I looked had everything to do with it for some people. Now, I had to consider the possibility that maybe they were right. I *had* passed for white, albeit unwittingly, more times than I even knew. My Black ancestry *was* invisible to some, which meant I had the option of leaving my neighbor guessing. Was I Portuguese? Yes. No. Maybe so. I had a *choice*. I could simply withhold information to guarantee my safety. My light skin gave me an undeniable privilege that darker-skinned Black people did not have.

I get to be Black because I am Black.

That was what I should have said to Mary at that moment in the seminar.

But now a seed of doubt was planted, and I had to wonder: Was that true?

Throughout my college years, I'd been raising my fist and marching to the beat of "Power to the People." Now, I was exhausted. Would I spend the rest of my life having to explain and justify who I was?

Then, something shifted. One day, I made my way across campus to Kresge College, where I found the writer Gloria Anzaldúa working on a doctorate in literature. Gloria called herself a "Chicana-Mexicana-mestiza." She had edited *This Bridge Called My Back: Writings by Radical Women of Color*, a seminal collection for Black and brown feminists that was mandatory reading in women's studies courses across the country. I also found Ekua Omosupe, an African American single mom from Mississippi. We three became friends and I was no longer alone.

"I'm putting together a new anthology," Gloria told me one day. "I was wondering if you have any essays or poems you'd like to contribute?" She did that thing that is so often missing from our lives as Black scholars and academics: *nurturing*. "It doesn't have to be polished. Just send me what you have." My essay, which I called "Light-Skinned-ded Naps," appeared in *Haciendo Caras: Making Face, Making Soul* the next year. It was my first published piece of writing. I was twenty-three years old.

Not long afterward, the literature department—which was not my department, mind you—brought the novelists Toni Cade Bambara and Buchi Emecheta to campus as distinguished visiting professors, and my life changed again. I became their teaching assistant, crossing campus regularly to commune with my newfound Black community.

One morning after class, I walked with Toni back to her office. The day was bright and impossibly blue, which made her next words seem incongruous. She pulled a small AM radio from her pocket. "Always carry a shortwave radio," she told me. "For when the revolution comes." I loved her commitment to revolutionary ideas, and to Black people.

And to me.

I plopped myself down in a chair in her office as we continued our conversation. Mostly, I was hungry for her affirmation, which she gave freely. Years later, I rediscovered an old cassette tape of an interview she gave for my dissertation, which was about nationalist desire in Black television, film, and literature. Playing it back, I was mortified to discover that I had done most of the talking. Toni listened patiently, offering "mm-hmms" and "hmms" in all the right places.

Even after leaving Santa Cruz, we continued to write to one another from time to time. Without my ever having to ask, she recommended me to a publisher and to a literary agent. She wondered how my dissertation was coming along and shared tidbits about her dating life. A few years later, I asked if she would contribute to a book of essays I was putting together. As gracious as ever, she said yes. I had no idea at the time that she was sick, and that she would, in fact, succumb to cancer within a matter of months.

With the Nigerian novelist Buchi Emecheta, one day in particular stands out in my memory. Buchi stood before a class of white students, pausing to survey a Douglas fir outside the window. "For you, the trees and the forest are very beautiful," she said. "Beau-ti-ful," she repeated, enunciating each syllable in her thick British accent. "But for me I see something more in the forests."

Uh-oh. I surveyed the room, sensing what was coming.

"I see fear and danger." She pronounced this last word "*dan*-jah," allowing it to linger in the coffee-scented air for a beat or two. "You just don't know who might be behind those trees." The class considered her words in silence. She was right, and they knew it, although I doubt that a Black person had ever said this to them before in quite that way.

"And, if something happens, well, then . . . I'm just another Black woman gone. I wouldn't even get two sentences in the newspaper." Buchi paused, allowing students to sit with their discomfort awhile. One rustled paper. Another crossed and uncrossed her legs.

Buchi smiled, shifting the mood. "Well . . . you know." Her expression turned playful. "Since I am Buchi, I might get two or three lines." A burst of relieved laughter.

The next year, two Latinas and another Black woman enrolled in my program. Since there was now a critical mass of students of color, we rallied and demanded that the department hire a Black woman professor, because that is precisely how these things work. There is power in numbers. The university heard our demands, and, in 1990, the scholar and activist Angela Davis became the first person of color ever to join the full-time faculty in the History of Consciousness program. She arrived just as I was leaving, and although I didn't get to take any classes with her, she supported me by serving on my dissertation committee. Later, I shivered with pride when she told me that my scholarship gave her a new perspective on television and that she could now see the value in examining constructions of race and gender in the sitcoms and dramas that I'd written about.

In 1990, I put on a black skirt and blazer and showed up for the oral defense of my dissertation proposal. My committee was stellar: feminist film theory scholar Teresa de Lauretis, sociologist Herman Gray, and Angela Davis.

"I'm interested in the ways in which you're configuring 'home' in Black television," Herman began. "Can you say more about that?" He was the coolest cat I knew in academia. I loved to hear him talk about race and representation on *The Cosby Show*. My work continued in the tradition he pioneered, taking deep dives into shows such as *The Fresh Prince of Bel-Air.* Why was Carlton depicted as not Black enough? And Uncle Phil? My scholarly arguments were the same as those that consumed my personal life. Who fits in? Who doesn't? Who's "authentically" Black? Writing about television was my attempt to make sense of my own reality. What's more, for the first time in television history, there were now Black directors, executive producers, and writers running prime-time shows, and these themes were everywhere in their work—on series from the 1990s, such as *Roc, New York Undercover,* and *South Central.*

"Thank you for that question." I paused, nervous. "I plan to use Benedict Anderson's notion of imagined communities to talk about how Black producers and creators continue to portray mythical configurations of 'home,' even as they simultaneously challenge the limits and contradictions of such a place." The committee members nodded, urging me forward.

"We continue to hold dear the mythical symbols of shared blackness. For example, Spike Lee's Africa pendant in red, black, and green; shared in-group references that are often revealed in improvised content and humor. However, creators also acknowledge that we are not all from the same place—that, try as we may to uphold and construct it, there is no one 'authentic' Black experience."

All my life I had yearned for the kind of Black community my mother and grandmother had in Chicago. A close-knit tribe that looked after one another. Like the Christmas Eve Mom told me about, when uncles and aunts and cousins showed up to their small apartment just as a blizzard hit. My grandmother's aunts Lish, Priscilla, Roxie, and Sarah and uncles George and Matthew partied all night, and by morning, not a single car was visible beneath the snow. Mom said the women and girls curled up in the only bed in the house, while the men and boys piled up on a let-out couch. They slept there, crowded together on that winter morning, and my mother said she had never felt so happy.

Blindly, I overlooked the hardship and suffering of my family's life on the South Side of Chicago and all the ways in which the "homes" of our imaginations had never been safe, unified spaces—not for women and girls, not for those with too-dark or too-light skin, not for those who didn't fit into heterosexual norms. Instead, I preferred to cling to the other side of that reality—to stories about how Black folks came together to help those in need at "rent parties" and how they watched over each other's children—all of which was also true. I especially loved to hear about how, when my grandfather was dying, friends and neighbors stopped by every payday Friday, offering Dra whatever money they could spare. When my family reminisced about Chicago, I (like those TV creators) heard tales of a mythical, imagined Black community that I longed to call my own.

After an hour or so, someone popped a champagne bottle and my professors stood to offer congratulatory hugs. It was official. I was ABD: "All but the dissertation." I may not have grasped every sentence written by theorists such as Mouffe and Laclau, but I had come a long way. My graduate training had changed me. I was intellectually stronger. Sharper.

My friend Nanci and a few others waited for me in the hallway. They let out a collective whoop when the door flung open and they saw my face. "You're free, girlfriend!" Nanci cried out. During my last years in the program, she and her partner, Yves, had provided the backbone of my emotional sustenance, opening their apartment and allowing me to make it my second home. We commiserated together as we watched CNN during Operation Desert Shield from their living room. We read and studied together and held each other's hands, laughing as Yves stirred fresh cumin seeds into one of his famous homemade Haitian dishes.

And now, Nanci was right. I was free to go anywhere. I could leave Santa Cruz and go back to Los Angeles at long last. Already, I had a list of Black television producers and writers that I hoped to interview for my dissertation. I was ready, itching to get started with my post–grad school life.

But another part of me was not free at all. The confused girl-child who needed answers was still there, inside. She lay in wait, ready to sabotage my best-laid plans if I refused to attend to her needs. Ultimately, she would succeed in getting my attention, as our shadows always do. Two years later, my unfinished dissertation pages would sit forgotten, along with my dreams of becoming a writer. They stayed there, discarded at the back of my closet, collecting dust, as I tried to piece together how my life had been derailed and where I had gone so terribly wrong.

detour

As I cruised north on Fairfax Avenue, a clunky, newfangled mobile phone rang from the console of my convertible Mazda Miata. Back in Los Angeles, I'd managed to fall into the high-paid world of medical interpreting. What started as a part-time gig to pay bills had, to my surprise, turned into a full-fledged business. Before I knew it, my company, which I called Zook & Associates, employed more than twenty part-time translators, working in a dozen or so languages.

The business had paid for a two-bedroom condominium in South Los Angeles, where I set up a home office and a couple of four-line phones. Susana, a young Latina mom, booked my appointments while I crisscrossed the city meeting with clients. It wasn't quite the life I'd planned, but I told myself it worked. I was making a good living, paying off my college debts.

"Where are you?" It was my boyfriend, Joe, on the phone. I'd recently invited him to move into my condo.

"Uh, Fairfax District. Why?" He sounded oddly suspicious.

"Just wondering."

The top was down on the convertible. I glanced in the rearview mirror, feeling strangely exposed.

"Where are *you*?" I asked.

"Oh. I'm around."

I had no idea what to make of his mysterious tone.

"Well, do you want to meet or something?" There was an Ethiopian restaurant nearby where we often went for dinner.

"Maybe."

"OK, let me know." I replaced the phone in the console and continued with my errands. I'd almost forgotten the call when a menacing figure suddenly appeared at my window. "Ah!" I gasped aloud. It was Joe, hovering over me in the middle of traffic. He wore a raincoat I had never seen before, despite the bright sunshine and cloudless sky.

"What are you doing? Are you following me?"

He laughed in a bizarre, detached way. Then he spoke to me slowly, almost as if he were possessed. "Why wouldn't you tell me where you were going, Kristal?"

I don't remember how the confrontation ended exactly, only that somehow, I managed to drive away from this demonic-looking apparition. Joe remained alone, standing in the middle of the street in his rain jacket.

Not long after his stalking incident, he arrived home bleary-eyed from a bar. Without a word of explanation, he set about yanking me around, shoving and pushing me and demanding to know where I'd been. Where *I'd* been? Out of nowhere, down came the palm of his hand across one of my cheeks, then the other. He pinned me to the bed, slapping my face again and again.

It was true that the men in my life had not treated me well, but this was a new low. No man had ever hit me before. Not as a child, and certainly not as a grown woman. In hindsight, the abuse could have been worse, physically. He hadn't used his fists, and other than some redness and swelling, I would be fine. And yet, he had violated my boundaries in profoundly meaningful ways. After this episode, Joe left the house as abruptly as he had arrived—headed back to the bars, I gathered. I hardly recognized myself as I slouched down to the kitchen and opened first one beer, then another. In the shower, I was surprised to discover shards of green glass from a broken bottle and blood seeping down the drain from a gash in my foot. I hadn't even felt the cut happen. Too numb and drunk to care, I slunk to the bottom of the tub.

I was never one to contemplate suicide. I was too much of an optimist for that. Still, at that moment, it was as though living with Joe, and everything that had conspired to get me there, had snapped a nerve. As I sat in my own blood, I remember distinctly thinking the following thoughts: *I've lived a good life. It would be OK to go now. I wouldn't mind. It would be good to just be done.*

Of course, I did not die. Giving up simply wasn't in my character.

In fact, the next morning I was back to being the strong Black woman Mom and Dra had raised. I had a plan. Now it was time to get down to business. First, I cleared every piece of Joe's clothing from the closet—his suits, ties, and dress shirts—and set them outside in a garbage bag. Next, I called a locksmith to change the dead bolt. Since Joe was in the same line of work as me, we also shared client referrals. I would have to take the hit. I had enough clients of my own, I decided. I'd be all right.

But through it all, a single thought repeated itself again and again in my mind, haunting me: *How had this happened? I had fallen for a drunk, a man just like my father. Why?* The question wouldn't let me rest. So, once again, as I had done so many times before, I reached for my father, whom I hadn't spoken to in years. Maybe he could help me make sense of what had happened. I decided to lay the situation out plainly and ask for help. It was the last thing on my to-do list for the day.

Exhaling, I dialed his number.

"I wanted to talk to you about some trouble I've been having lately," I began.

"OK, sure." My father was an experienced twelve-steps sponsor on Vashon Island. He didn't give advice, as he often said. Instead, his role was to listen to those in need and to share his own experiences, which he'd been doing for many years as a long-standing sober member of the twelve-steps community.

I dove in headlong, confessing every single last humiliating detail about Joe and me.

"Huh." I could almost hear my father nodding through the phone, digesting my words. "Well, sweetheart. I've found that it's important to have a spiritual practice before getting into a relationship with someone, and to know whether or not they have a spiritual practice of their own."

Of course, he was right. But neutral advice wasn't what I needed. I wasn't one of his sponsees. I was his *daughter*. And I'd just told him that a man had *hit me*. I wanted my father to rush in to protect and console me in all the ways he'd never done. I wanted him to hold my hand and walk me through this deadly minefield of intimacy. Couldn't he see that I had no idea how to trust men? Or myself? Couldn't he see that I needed him to step up and show me that it was still possible?

Six years had passed since I had first written to my father in search of a deeper connection. Six years of fumbling and stuttering between us, and still, we were no closer than when we had begun.

The house was quiet now without Joe. I was alone. Free. Although I was earning six figures with my business—more than I'd ever made in my life—the small voice inside of me knew that Zook & Associates was never meant to be my calling. That was when I made a life-changing decision. I disconnected the business lines in the second bedroom and packed away my company brochures.

It was over.

I reached into the back of the closet and pulled out stacks of notes from my unfinished dissertation, laying the pages across the two office desks. I began writing on a chilly November morning and didn't stop until New Year's Day. During breaks, I hung colorful new artwork on the walls and set towering palm trees and ficus plants in every corner. I wrote for my life. I wrote from my heart.

That winter, my dissertation committee approved my work with glowing praise. After ten years of college, I was done. Soon, I would graduate with a PhD.

Once again, I dialed my father's number.

"Are you sitting down?" I asked when he picked up.

"Yes?"

I smiled, stirring batter for pancakes in my kitchen. I'd been out on a date the night before. Single life was treating me well. Gradually, my still low self-esteem was at least returning to pre-Joe levels.

"I finished the dissertation! I'll be getting my PhD soon!"

My father whooped with joy. "Wow! That's terrific. Congratulations!"

"Yeah. And . . . well, I thought maybe you'd like to come to the ceremony?"

My father thought for a moment. "In Santa Cruz?"

"Yeah."

He let out another whoop. "Yeah! I'd love to do that!"

I could hear the emotion in his voice as he began making plans, wondering aloud how he could "get an airplane to take him" to California. I had to smile at this. In all of my father's wild adventures, it struck me that the one thing he'd not done much of was flying on an airplane.

"I'm really looking forward to seeing you," he added before hanging up. "Thank you for including me."

In solidarity with several Black classmates, I wore a kente cloth sash draped across my chest, together with my cap and gown. That day, I would take my first photo ever with my parents. To my right, my mother smiled, wearing braided extensions and oversize sunglasses. To my left was my father in a dress shirt and tie. We must have all been feeling so much in that moment, yet saying so little about it. The truth was, it was a lot to absorb. I was meeting my father for the first time as an adult and receiving my PhD on the same day.

After snapping a few more photos, we piled into cars headed over the mountain to San Jose, where family and friends filled my uncle Arthur and aunt Kitty's home, spilling into the backyard and congregating around the grill. A friend from high school, Carolyn, had made the trip north to help celebrate, as had my dear friend Monique, who had seen me through the difficult Joe years. I felt truly blessed to be surrounded by so much love.

During a quiet moment away from the crowd, my father pulled me aside and handed me an envelope.

"This is for you."

In it, I found a check for $1,000 with a note written on the hotel stationery from the place he'd stayed the night before. He began by giving "praise and honor" to Mom and Dra, and to God, and reminding me never to forget "where all blessings originate."

I have not experienced your ups and downs with you. Nor have I been there to comfort and encourage you. However, I have always been with you spiritually and I always will be with you in spirit.

"Thank you." I hugged my father, placing the check and note in my bag. I certainly appreciated the money, given the mountain of debt I had in college loans. It would provide a much-needed respite from my financial worries. I could see that, with it, my father was again trying to make amends. But something was missing. What did he mean when he said he would always be with me *in spirit*? I wondered. I needed him to stick around in the flesh. Could he do that? Did he want to? The frightened little girl in me had a hard time taking his words on faith.

Earlier, he and my mother had slipped out together to take a walk and smoke. It was their first time alone together in decades.

"What did you and my mom talk about?"

"I told her that I never meant to leave her."

His answer floored me. "What do you mean?"

He shook his head. "I was high. I didn't know what I was doing. I think I got on a bus and went to San Francisco."

I stared at him. "So why didn't you go back later?"

There was a long pause between us until, finally, he chuckled, and again shook his head. "I don't know."

"I told her that she was the love of my life," he continued. "I don't think she believed me, though."

I didn't know what to believe either.

"What about Michele?" He had been happily married to his second wife for more than twenty years.

"I wouldn't be here today if it wasn't for Michele. She's the reason I'm alive. But your mom was different."

I knitted my brows. "And what did my mother say to that?"

"She said that the reason we were put together was to have you." He held my gaze. "We talked about you and your childhood. Your mom told me that my being gone had a deep effect on you." He crooked his neck slightly, as if to shake off some discomfort. "She said it affected you much more than she thought it would at the time."

I said nothing to this. What was there to say?

Only much later would I piece together the full story.

My mother was pregnant with me when my father walked out of their Los Angeles apartment for the last time on a whirlwind spree of addiction. He ended up in a drug-filled Victorian home in the Haight-Ashbury district of San Francisco, where he took a hundred doses of LSD in a single pop. "That's how I missed a decade of my life," he would later say.

It wasn't an exaggeration.

My father, literally, did not know where he'd been or what he'd done for a period of years. He would go to Chinatown and talk to people in what he thought was perfect Chinese. He was "totally and completely insane," as he put it. When he was unable to string together any kind of coherent statement in a courtroom, a judge remanded him to a padded cell at Atascadero State Mental Hospital in San Luis Obispo County, where he probably belonged.

In 1970, when I was five, the state saw fit to institutionalize my father again, this time in the alcoholism ward of the Camarillo State Mental Hospital. Michele, a nurse several years older than my mother, was divorced, with two sons of her own. She told my father that alcoholism was a disease—a *sickness*. This time, something in him finally heard the words, and he understood. Michele became his anchor. They held fast to each other and didn't let go.

"When are you leaving?" he asked.

"Tomorrow. What about you?"

"Well, I planned to fly back to Seattle today but I talked to my sponsor about it, and he told me to change the ticket."

"Oh? Why?"

What my father said next would send me reeling, crashing through my defenses. He studied me closely before responding.

"He told me that, for once, I should be the one to watch you go. Not the other way around. He said you shouldn't have to watch me leave again."

I pushed back a wall of bitter tears.

"I thought it made a lot of sense," my father continued. "So, I'm staying right here. I'm not going anywhere until you do."

Out of all the things my father said and did that day, it was this small gesture that broke me—a comment and a decision that would stay with me always. His effort to avoid causing me further pain helped me to lay down my armor just that much more. Those simple words and that choice urged me forward, allowing me to believe in his good intentions.

My father later told me that he cried all the way from the Seattle airport to the Vashon Island ferry. He had to stop driving to dry his glasses. Were they tears of joy? Regret? Both? I couldn't be sure. A thousand questions swirled in my mind. If I hadn't looked for him, would he have been content never knowing me? And what about now? He loved me, but would his love be consistent? Inside, I was still that eager little girl with her bleeding heart splattered across the floor. Was I just setting her up for another fall? Maybe one day, I would have to look for my father again—only to discover that he was nowhere to be found.

writer

I gathered my articles and essays into a folder and trekked to the office of the *LA Weekly* in Silver Lake, hoping to break into the paper. Getting my PhD was an honor, but I wanted to be a writer, not a professor. For me, the words came first. Pen to page. Fingers to keyboard. Writing was where I felt most alive.

"Too academic." Judith Lewis, arts editor for the *Weekly*, sat across from me at her desk, tearing through my tortured book review with a red Sharpie. She handed the pages back to me.

"The ideas are interesting, though." She thought for a moment. "Could you get me a revision in the next few days? Without the jargon?"

I glanced at the bleeding pages. "Sure. No problem."

Some months earlier, a friend had introduced me to Ed Boyle, an African American reporter with the *Los Angeles Times* who ran *ACCENT LA*, a small, community start-up newspaper, out of a home office in South L.A. Ed forgave my clichés and allowed me to contribute, giving me my first real bylined clips. I wrote about the annual Watts Festival, reviewed a

Neville Brothers album, and covered *Boyz N the Hood*, a little-known film directed by a twenty-three-year-old named John Singleton. A year later, Singleton would become the first African American and the youngest person ever to be nominated for the Academy Award for Best Director.

My postgraduate training in critical thinking made my journalism richer, deeper. Everything I'd learned about cultural studies and theory was woven into my reporting, which, I believe, gave it something of an edge, making it different from other arts reviews. Judith published my revision of that book review (without the jargon) and several more after that. Before long, I was a regular contributor to the *Weekly*. Later, she introduced me to film editor Manohla Dargis, and I wrote for her too. I was contributing so many articles to the paper, in fact, that when I went to buy stamps at the post office, a Black man working there recognized my name.

"Are you Kristal Brent Zook?"

I stood a little taller in my shoes. "Yes."

"Oh, wow. I love your stuff."

I walked out of there feeling like I'd made it. That's it, I thought, giddy with joy. *I'm famous.* I was ready for the big time. It was time to go to New York.

Preston Kevin Lewis, a friend of Nanci and Yves, offered me a mattress on the floor of the Fort Greene apartment he shared with his fiancée, Cari. I camped out there for two weeks, hoping to break into the *Village Voice*. Personal laptops and internet cafés were not yet a thing for struggling writers like me, so I set up shop in a computer lab at Barnard College.

Stepping over used drug needles in the snow, I rode the number 2 subway to Harlem each morning, where I would piece together story ideas and then cart my pitches—a stack of dot matrix printouts—downtown to the *Voice*. The writer Nelson George introduced me to arts editor Lisa Kennedy, who saw something in my notes and eventually gave me my first assignment: a Q&A with George Jackson and Doug McHenry, producers of *House Party 2* and *New Jack City*.

By the time I made my second foray to New York, I was writing regularly for the *Voice* and even had enough cash for a rented PowerBook and several nights at the Gramercy Park Hotel. I worked hard, joyfully, lulled by the hum and burr of the AC on a sticky summer afternoon, delighting in the clickety-clack sound of my fingers on the laptop.

Skipping around town, I reported on a Houston Baker lecture at Long Island University, a Black Popular Culture conference at the Dia Center for the Arts, and the annual National Black Writers Conference at CUNY's Medgar Evers College. My clip portfolio grew thick with essays, mostly about television and film: the first Korean American sitcom, the first woman captain in the *Star Trek* franchise, a controversial art exhibit about Black men. I went from talking breastfeeding with Jada Pinkett Smith to answering critics of Magic Johnson after he ventured into the role of late-night talk show host.

My first big breaking news story was the 1992 L.A. uprisings that erupted after the four police officers who beat Rodney King were set free. They had crushed his ribs and skull and caused him permanent brain damage. It was the first time the entire world had witnessed such police brutality up close, after a bystander recorded it on video. Lisa Kennedy, my editor at the *Voice*, called from New York to ask if I might write about what some were calling the L.A. "riots." As we talked, I stood on the balcony of my Inglewood condo, watching smoke rise across the horizon.

"Could you get some quotes?" Lisa wanted to know. "Find out what people are thinking and feeling?"

It was a chance to move into hard news. I was nervous, excited, and more than ready. I started off easy, venturing a few miles east to Simply Wholesome, a Black-owned vegetarian restaurant on Slauson Avenue. I was a regular there and figured I could start by talking to the owner, Percell Keeling, whom I'd profiled for the *Los Angeles Times Magazine*. When I arrived, I saw that across the street from the restaurant, protestors had smashed the windows of the Korean-owned dry cleaners where I sent my clothes. All across the city, Fruit of Islam security detail fanned out, on twenty-four-hour watch patrolling Black businesses.

Percell was busy with customers, but he found a quiet moment and we sat at one of the tables to talk. He studied me carefully before beginning, though.

"Listen, Kristal . . ." There was concern in his eyes.

"Yeah. What's up?" My notebook and pen were at the ready.

"It's just . . . I don't know how to say this." I could tell he was trying to make a point as gently as he could. "Should you really be out here? You know what I'm saying? Not everybody out here knows you're Black."

I did know what he was saying.

Not far away, at the corner of Florence and Normandie, Black protestors had dragged Reginald Denny, a white truck driver, from his cab and beaten him to a pulp. Denny was in the wrong place at the wrong time. Just the night before, in fact, I'd been terrified myself, sitting in my car watching as several young men smashed a streetlight just a few yards away. "White man made that light!" one of them shouted. I decided that Percell was right. I was twenty-seven years old and not ready to die. I decided to make some calls and write the essay from home.

As a journalist, I remained especially intrigued by the topics of race and mixed race, reviewing the film *Listen Up*, a documentary about music producer Quincy Jones, who had been married three times to three white women. Back then, seeing biracial people on-screen was still unusual. Jones's daughter Rashida was not yet on *The Office*, just as Maya Rudolph was not yet on *Saturday Night Live* and Tracee Ellis Ross was not yet on *Black-ish*. I yearned to know more about the experiences of biracial children and their families, but that kind of widespread awareness was still decades away.

For another story, I trekked to Camden, New Jersey, to the home of Kristin Hunter, whose novels featured light-skinned protagonists. Literary critic Claudia Tate had called Hunter "one of the most neglected black women writers in the country."

I wanted to know why.

Kristin and her husband, John Lattany, received me warmly, laying out smoked salmon, pita bread, and cantaloupe slices for lunch. "You remind me of myself when I was young," she confided as we sipped hot tea. Leaning across the table, she added, "Do you think I'm obsessed with color?"

I laughed. "Maybe. A little. But then, so am I."

She was gracious and grateful to have her work highlighted. But there was more to her story, said Kristin's husband, John, as he drove me back to the train station that evening. He was troubled by what his wife had *not* said during our interview. Lattany told me that the literary establishment had treated Hunter very badly indeed. "There are Black writers' conferences where she hasn't been allowed to speak, and anthologies with Blacker-than-thou attitudes that have shut her out completely." His hands trembled with emotion. "You have to understand. There has been a whole slew of attacks against her from Black people."

"Why?" I asked.

He shrugged, exasperated. "Some of them resent her light skin. Some accuse her of trying to speak for the masses. That's not what she's doing. She's just speaking her truth."

Lattany's words would be prescient. A warning siren. The message was clear: light-skinned women should not claim to have too much authority on the subject of blackness. I should have paid more attention to what Lattany was telling me. Soon, I would have to learn this lesson for myself.

The hard way.

Every life has its moment when everything changes. It may come in a letter or an email. Or perhaps it shows up as a knock at the door. For me, that instant when my life would be divided into "before" and "after" came with a phone call. It was the summer of 1995, and I had just finished an article for the *Village Voice*, faxing it off to New York. Stretching, I crossed the hall to my bedroom just as the phone on my nightstand rang. It was 5 p.m. in Los Angeles. After hours on the East Coast.

"Hi, my name is Veronica Chambers. I'm trying to reach Kristal Brent Zook?" Veronica was a twentysomething Afro-Latina editor at the *New York Times Sunday Magazine*, the first Black woman ever to serve in that position.

I bumbled out some kind of reply. "Hi. That's me."

"I've read your work in the *LA Weekly*," she continued, "and wanted to know if you'd be interested in writing an article for us?"

The sky opened above me. Angels sang.

"We'd like to do a piece about Black feminism, to explore what it looks and feels like today." I couldn't believe it. It was my dream assignment. I couldn't have picked a topic dearer to my heart.

"Uh, yeah," I managed. "I'd love to."

Over the next several weeks, Veronica and I hammered out the details of my assignment. I drafted a pitch that she tweaked. After a few revisions, the proposal was ready to be shared with Veronica's top editors, who approved wholeheartedly. We launched forward. The story would take me first to Minneapolis, to report on the annual NAACP conference, with the aim of getting a glimpse into contemporary women's leadership in that venerable civil rights organization. Next, I was sent to Washington, DC, for the Million Man March, an event spearheaded by Minister Louis Farrakhan that aimed to unite and strengthen Black men and communities.

My reporting goal was to shift the spotlight, even for just a moment, away from those "Great Heroes" T-shirts that I had seen lately on the chests of so many Black men—the faces of Malcolm, Martin, Marcus, Mandela, and Marley all huddled together in a cluster. As beloved as they were, to me and to everyone else, I wanted to reframe the view from that male mountaintop—to make room for the Anita Hills of the world, and the Joycelyn Elderses, and the Jo Ann Robinsons, and so many other women who had never been a part of our collective consciousness.

While admiring its intent, I disagreed strongly with the march's patriarchal foundations, as did other prominent feminist figures, such as Angela Davis. In fact, when I first told Angela about the upcoming march in a phone call, I remember her saying that she wished more young women would stand up and speak, and that activists like herself would prefer to pass the baton to the next generation. I took this in, the idea that this was a new time and that there was a need for a shift in thinking about Black feminism.

"A Manifesto of Sorts for a Black Feminist Movement" was the headline my editors chose, and I thought it worked well. I saw that Veronica had been right to highlight this topic, which was so timely in 1995. After a jury had found O. J. Simpson not guilty on the charges of murdering his wife, Nicole Brown Simpson, and her friend Ron Goldman, Simpson remained a celebrated figure in Black communities despite a history of domestic violence. "GUILTY OR NOT, WE LOVE YOU, O. J." read a placard held up by Black women.

That same year, boxing heavyweight champion Mike Tyson received a hero's welcome in Harlem after serving three years on a rape charge. It was twenty years before #MeToo, and sexual harassment, assault, and violence within Black communities were still considered "dirty laundry" that should not be aired to the public. African Americans refrained from discussing such truths with broader audiences, and many would not ap-prove of this kind of revelation in the venerable pages of the *New York Times*. Writing about Black-on-Black violence, there, in that way, was risky in ways that I did not yet appreciate. I was naive, to say the least.

I spent months on the article, laboring over every word. Once, I remember falling into a coma-like sleep for twelve hours, during which I seem to have dreamed of every single sentence and paragraph, anguishing over the precise phrasing and intonation of each word. Around and around the copy went in my mind. But for all my hard work and good intentions, I made one crucial mistake: I tried to do it alone.

In hindsight, I could have used more eyes on the controversial ideas I was laying down.

Although I knew several Black writers, in many ways, I was a professional loner. Why didn't I share some of my thoughts with some of the Black women and men who had so carefully nurtured and mentored me along the way, such as my high school journalism teacher, Gail Spann, or my college mentor, Professor Butler-Evans, or Lynell George, who had helped me get my foot in the door at the *LA Weekly*, or the first person to hire me as an adjunct professor, Valerie Smith at UCLA? Instead, my pride prevailed.

I thought I had this one in the bag.

A friend who was no stranger to the spotlight himself loved the piece but took care to warn me. "Be ready," he said. "The attacks will be personal."

I was too excited to pay him much mind.

Diane Cardwell, a new editor at the magazine, also Black, called to ask if she could send a photographer to my home. Why not? I thought blithely. Posing in my living room, I wore a sleek pencil skirt and a knowing expression, unaware of what my image might mean in the context of what I had just written. I was wearing my hair long at the time, chemically relaxed and blow-dried just so. Against the background of my green eyes and light skin, my proclamations about what Black feminism was, or should be, must have seemed odd to some. If I didn't yet understand the power of art and images to frame a story's arguments, it was a lesson I was about to learn.

The spread included a checkerboard of close-ups depicting three generations of Black women—those we called the "old guard," respected widow-queens who had initially earned their titles because of the men they had married; intellectuals who had pioneered theories of intersectionality, such as Angela Davis and UCLA law professor Kimberlé Crenshaw; and a third row of faces depicting a new generation of activists and writers, such as Rebecca Walker and, as it turned out (surprise!), me. There I was, front and center: part of a new feminist guard that would take over and finally set things right.

Huh? That was not at all what I had written.

I wasn't even an activist anymore—not in that way—and the story certainly wasn't about me. But the images were more powerful than the words. The article was met with both praise and profound criticism. Responses hit me like a sidelong pummeling. *Who is she to speak for Black people? She's not even Black her own damn self.* The blows took me down. Hard. Despite receiving an especially cherished note from the writer June Jordan, thanking me for the piece, I had to consider the possibility that maybe my critics were right. Perhaps I had no right to speak—at least not in that way, in that forum.

When the flurry of cable television appearances eventually petered out, I tried to dust myself off by getting back to my activist roots. Somehow, I felt the need to prove that I was more than just a journalist, that I was an advocate, too.

I volunteered at Metropolitan Continuation High School for at-risk kids, but that attempt fell flat. I wasn't even sure why. My attempts to get the youth excited about words drew blank stares. The girls focused on applying their mascara and thick blue eye shadow instead.

Next, I resolved to be a Big Sister to a twelve-year-old biracial girl, another effort that failed miserably. On our first day out, I treated my charge to breakfast at IHOP to break the ice. It had been my favorite restaurant as a child, and I hoped that the comfort food would have the same effect on her that it had always had on me. Who knows, maybe we both needed comfort that day. But she stared at me across a pile of chocolate chip pancakes with a dull look in her eyes.

"Is this it?"

"Is what it?"

"Is this all we're going to do today?"

I stammered a reply. "Well, I don't know. Was there something else you wanted to do?"

She sighed. "I guess not."

My Little Sister later confessed that she had expected more from me in the way of gifts. Cash, really, to be precise. She had heard that was what Big Sisters did, she said, which was why she signed up in the first place. We got past this hurdle—or so I thought—and I took her on outings to the mountains and to the beach. But our connection never quite jelled. After what I'd just been through with the *Times* article, I took the failure personally, as though I was somehow not quite good enough.

"I'm beginning to see what you do," my father wrote after reading my work. "There is so much fear in this world that one can replace with love, if only we knew how." He called my words a "light in the darkness" and I drank in his praise. "Keep up the good work and I will always love you," he wrote. Then, thinking better of it, he added: "P.S. I will always love you even if you *don't* keep up the good work." I reread that last line five times, bursting into tears. I *was* working for love: love from my parents, from men, from Black people. I was a workaholic, in fact. Work was my passion as well as my drug of choice.

But was it possible that I might be able simply to stop trying so hard and just *be*?

Someone had once told me that crystal creates rainbows by slowing and bending light. I desperately wanted to embody my name, to be the kind of person who could bend and slow light—shaping perceptions and creating rainbows. But despite my efforts to be a voice, I was not there. Not yet. Not by a long shot.

pain

"How many hours a day do you work?" Michele Moy was an acupuncturist at Emperor's College of Traditional Oriental Medicine in Santa Monica. She stood beside me with a clipboard, documenting my symptoms.

How many hours?

To my surprise, I couldn't come up with an answer.

There was never a beginning or end to my workdays. Activity went from as soon as I could get up in the morning until as long as I could last at night. For every lucrative assignment I received, there were three times as many rejections. To my mind, I was never productive enough, prepared enough. Smart enough.

"I don't know," I finally answered. "A lot."

I had developed chronic back pain, which started somewhere in the thoracic region and now radiated along the entire right side of my body, from neck to hip. Already I'd tried the Alexander Technique, Pilates, yoga, massages, physical therapy, and strength training. I had seen orthopedic surgeons, chiropractors, psychics, astrologers, herbalists, and naturopaths. I had given myself white willow bark tea and Saint-John's-wort, and rubbed myself down with sandalwood oil.

Nothing helped.

Michele examined my tongue. I liked how she was both Chinese and American at once, at home with both the Eastern and Western sides of herself. Her fingers grazed the rhomboid muscle between my scapula and the spine.

"How long have you had this pain?"

"A year. Maybe two."

She sat down at the foot of the examination bed; her hip pressed against my calf. "You have yin deficiency," she said. I had no idea what she was talking about. She smiled, taking in my confused expression. "Yin is the side of us that provides nurturing and tenderness." Again, it was as though she spoke in a foreign language.

Nurturing?

"Yes. It means there's a lack of nourishment and self-care."

My chest constricted. I knew in my heart that her diagnosis was one thousand percent correct. Often, I ignored hunger pangs during the day, fueling them with coffee. My problem wasn't food. I loved eating. My problem was feeling that I didn't deserve to stop working long enough to enjoy a relaxed meal. Even out with friends, I often stuck to snacks— appetizers and wine. Full plates were too expensive. Just a bite and a couple of drinks would do.

"Think of yin deficiency as a misunderstanding between action and sur- render," Michele said. "You push yourself to work harder when you should curl up and rest. Other times, you give up too soon when what's really needed is a good fight." Her insight was so accurate it stopped me cold.

She inserted tiny needles in my arms, legs, stomach, ears, and scalp. "The pain you have is connected to your heart," she added, flicking the light switch off. "Now rest." She closed the door and left me alone in the dark.

There is a point on the outer ear where acupuncturists believe the spirit can be touched directly—something like a portal to the other side of consciousness. Michele had left needles there too. Thirty minutes later, I felt like I had traveled to the depths of the ocean in an airtight womb.

Even today, it is difficult to describe the feeling of absolute serenity that I felt after the treatment.

"I had . . . some kind of a vision," I told Michele when she came back into the room. My entire body was heavy with relaxation. Again, she sat on the examining bed beside me. I couldn't imagine having an experience even remotely like this with a Western physician—it felt like therapy, but deeper.

"Tell me about it," said Michele.

"Well . . . there was a medieval castle with a long corridor and a bridge. A latch floor trap led to dungeons and dark water below. Then, a voice asked how I would cross to the other side. So I answered, 'With you.' That's when the entire floor collapsed. There was nothing to stand on but dark space. At first, I wasn't sure what to do. But the voice said, simply: 'Leap of faith.'"

I left the clinic feeling as if my shoes were made of fluffy white clouds. Steering my Mazda Miata onto Cloverfield Boulevard, I knew immediately what had to be done. Memories rushed at me as I headed down Kansas Avenue, toward the apartment building of my childhood. I parked and, once inside the courtyard, studied the row of names on a stucco wall of mailboxes. In my wildest nightmares, I never expected to find his name there, two decades later. And yet, there he was: NOCHE #212.

My body had a will of its own, flying up the pebbled staircase. Before I knew what was happening, my hand had already made a fist and pounded on the door. Mrs. Noche answered with a quizzical expression. Where was he? I planned to ask. My adrenaline raced with rage, and I was loaded for bear. But Mrs. Noche's fragile appearance gave me pause. She was smaller and somehow more frail than I'd remembered her.

"Buenos días," I began, measuring my emotions. "Soy Kristal. La nina que vivía aquí hace muchos años."

I'm the little girl who lived here a long time ago.

There was a flash of recognition. "Ah, Kristal!" She pronounced my name Kree-stahl. "Sí! ¿Como estás?"

As she ushered me inside, I scanned the small apartment with eagle eyes. "¿Está Lina?"

Mrs. Noche looked surprised. She told me that her younger sister was married now and had been living in North Carolina for many years.

"¿Y su marido?"

And your husband? Where is he?

She paused, again seemingly taken off guard. "Oh," she suddenly said, in English. "He had lot of problems." She pressed her hand to her chest, inhaling. "We separated long time ago."

I studied Mrs. Noche more closely. *What kind of problems?* I wanted to ask. *Did you know that he was a child molester? Did he molest your own children? Your grandchildren? Did he molest Lina?* I wanted to confront him in person. To beat him down. To send him away for a long time.

But just as a question formed on my lips, a young man with a toothy grin burst through the door. Victor, the Noches' youngest son, had been an infant when we moved away. Now, tattoos and military muscles peeked out from beneath his white T-shirt. I imagined what it would be like to say the words to them both: *Victor, your father assaulted me. He stole my girlhood. Stole my innocence. Tell me where he is. I need to find him, now.* But something stopped me. I could not do it. Not to him. Not to his mother. Anyway, the perpetrator was gone now, I reasoned. What more was there to say?

The truth was, there was a lot more to say.

I simply wasn't ready to say it.

Instead, I went home, changed into workout clothes, and drove to my favorite stretch of beach at Playa del Rey, where I often jogged a mile or two. Afterward, I stopped to stare at the sunset, whispering supplications to the clouds. On this particular day, though, I was distracted by an unexpected sight.

Halfway through my run, I noticed that an injured bird had drifted in with the tide and was being terrorized by a flock of seagulls that pecked violently at his not-yet-dead carcass on the beach. I wanted to swoop down and wrap him in my sweatshirt so that he could die a peaceful death, but he squawked at me with such red-beaked force that I backed away.

The analogy seemed fitting.

Better to die at the hands of the known than to be saved by an unknown force.

I, too, was screeching red-beaked in the sand, just like that injured bird.

I didn't want to die, but at the same time, something in me found the idea of survival and a new way of life terrifying.

That's precisely when unknown forces of my own swooped in to save me.

Dra and Mom in Chicago

• • •

Dad as a young man

Opposite:

Mexican train with
family and close friend
Monique

• • •

Wedding day with Maria

This page:

On vacation with
Alfonso

• • •

Miami book club
friends

The adoption is final

• • •

Mommy and Olivia

Dad and Olivia meet
for the first time

• • •

Mom, Lisa, and
Olivia at the beach

Dra in later years

● ● ●

Mom and me

australia

I remember a thousand reverent moments from the year 1996: sitting outside my loft apartment with a cup of Madura tea watching rain clouds; an isolated oceanside cabin and crashing waves; crisp Granny Smith apples and fresh Swiss cheese. I remember long jogs with summer raindrops caressing my skin, lavender-scented bathwater in an antique claw bathtub, and the utter absence of clocks or watches. I remember raging purple sunsets. I remember a vase of gardenias on my kitchen counter before bedtime.

That summer, I moved to the upside-down land of Australia.

It was July, their winter season, when I arrived on the far west coast, in the city of Perth, which was about as far from America as I could possibly be. A professor acquaintance from New York University had recommended me for a position teaching cultural studies at Murdoch University. After what I'd been through with the *New York Times* article, the offer couldn't have come at a better time. I was desperate to flee.

With the fifteen-hour time difference plus a layover in Sydney, my total travel time from Los Angeles was three days. I was exhausted and yet, at the same time, strangely energized. I quickly rented and settled into a cozy apartment and began a new routine. Each morning, upon opening my eyes, I took time to wonder at the wide, blue sky and how it relinquished any notion of a horizon. The terrain felt infinite. It was as though the land itself made space for my thoughts and emotions to expand, too. Instead of rushing to my desk and leaping into work as I usually did, I sat up in bed for several moments to study the maple tree outside my window, to breathe, and to pray. My prayers were basic, in the best sense of the word. *Show me. Lead me. Guide me. Heal me. Thank you.*

This new practice worked miracles on my psyche. Over time, mundane concerns took a back seat to wonderment. Intuition expanded. Premonitions became the norm. I found that logic was the least important part of my existence. The landscape was having a strange effect on me, indeed. Could it be that I had flung myself halfway across the globe just to learn how to sit still? I wondered. I prayed every day, listening closely for the next choice. The next revelation. Clearly, unknown forces had swooped down to rescue me. What I didn't know was that my road to salvation was only just beginning.

The course at Murdoch was the largest class I'd ever taught, with 244 students in an auditorium and six teaching assistants to share the load. The work was demanding, but I enjoyed shoring up all the obscure theories I'd only partially learned in graduate school. Even work felt different this time. Back home I'd been trying to sell articles, trying to be a mentor, trying to write a book, trying to make a name for myself, trying to be a race woman, trying to heal my back pain, trying to fix my relationship with my father, trying to earn my mother's approval. Trying, trying, and trying. But it was never enough. *I* was never enough. Now, I took a sabbatical from perfection.

In Australia, life became simple.

Forgiving.

One morning, the wife of a Nyungah colleague called, inviting me to join them and their two teenage daughters on a weekend getaway to Yallingup, a haven of clear blue water on the Indian Ocean. There was going to be an Aboriginal surf competition that weekend, she said. It would be fun. I packed an overnight bag within minutes.

At Yallingup, we roasted chicken and potatoes over an open fire and swam in the ocean. We explored hidden caves and licked ice cream cones that dripped onto our arms and bathing suits in the sweltering heat. At Yallingup, I fell in love with Damien, a free-spirited artist who had entered the surf competition. The son of an Italian and German father and a mother of Narangga and Pitjantjatjara descent, he had grown up as the only non-white kid in his classrooms. I learned that, at seventeen, he had also gone looking for the white father he never knew—a history that we had in common.

Dating a "black fellah," as they called themselves down under, forced me to reexamine lifelong assumptions about race from a new angle. The view from the Southern Hemisphere was nothing like what I'd known in America. Turning on the television at night, viewers might catch prime-time news stories about the Ugandan election or a Zambian harvest destroyed by locusts. Afterward, there might be a documentary about the Tiwi people of Melville Island. The world became larger as my mental and physical points of reference expanded exponentially.

During long conversations with Damien's mother, I learned that she had been one of Australia's "stolen children," forcibly taken from her family by the government during the 1950s and sent to orphanages for the purpose of being integrated into white culture. My time in Australia taught me to see the experiences of Black and brown people through global eyes—so much so that it would be difficult, once I was back home, to refocus my lens in the old familiar ways.

I awoke in a panic in the middle of the night, drenched in sweat. It took me a moment to realize that I was no longer in my peaceful apartment in Perth, Australia. My six-month teaching job had ended, and although I was offered a permanent, tenure-track position at Murdoch, I turned it down, eager to return to my writing career. So here I was, back in America, thousands of miles away, in a hotel room in Aspen, Colorado, preparing to interview actor/director Keenen Ivory Wayans at the HBO Comedy Festival.

My emotions were spinning.

Damien and I took turns making the twenty-hour trip (plus eighteen-hour time difference) back and forth during our now long-distance romance. He'd come to California for a month or two. I'd do the same, traveling to his home at the beach in Adelaide. We talked about one of us moving, but it never quite seemed to be the right decision. Damien was in serious culture shock when he visited Los Angeles, and I just couldn't imagine giving up the career I'd worked so long and hard to establish. The internet really wasn't a thing yet—personal email was just beginning to become common—and Australia was simply too isolated from the professional world of media that I lived in.

Still shell-shocked by my awakening in Aspen, I wrapped a blanket over my pajamas, slid open a balcony door, and sucked in the night air. Pristine, snow-covered mountains shone brightly against the dark sky. How did I get to this place? I wondered. I had come so far, only to feel like I was right back where I'd started. Once again, I was living in an in-between place, struggling to settle in, psychically, between vastly different cultures and landscapes. I wasn't willing to relocate to a foreign country permanently but found it difficult to be fully present back home in America. I was in limbo. Something inside me had shifted. I didn't know exactly what to do next, but I felt certain that I wasn't meant to continue along the same path as before.

On the heels of the *New York Times* article, a dozen publishers had made book offers. Before going to Australia, I'd signed a contract with one of them, agreeing to write a nonfiction exploration of Black feminism in America. The publisher would wait, they said, until my return. Now, it was time to get back to work. For my initial reporting, I focused on Sarah White, a Southern catfish plant laborer who, in the 1990s, led the largest strike of Black women workers ever to take place in the state of Mississippi. Her story was fascinating to me, and I couldn't believe that so few people knew about her.

But there was a problem. Sarah had no interest in "feminism," either as a word or as a movement. The way I saw it, I could force my editor's angle on her, or I could let Sarah tell her own story. The thought of having my loyalty questioned by Black people yet again was too much to bear. I could not take that risk, and more importantly, I did not want to. I decided not to engage in an analysis of the white feminist movement and, instead, to let Sarah's story speak for itself.

"I have some bad news for you, Kristal."

My literary agent was on the phone. Apparently, my editor wasn't happy with the Sarah White chapter that I'd submitted. "She wants to cancel the book," my agent said, wasting no time.

I sank into my chair. "Why?"

I could almost hear her shrug. My agent and I also parted ways not long afterward.

The perfect storm became a category five hurricane. Everything I touched in my writing career fell apart. A huge magazine feature was canceled due to lack of advertising. Another was postponed. Yet another was delayed indefinitely. It was a monumental streak of bad luck. No one would have guessed it from my Kenneth Cole leather jacket and chunky silver rings, but some days I didn't even have gas money. Finances were a constant stress, manifesting in thoughts like "Maybe I should just have a peanut butter sandwich for dinner tonight." Or "Can I really afford cream-colored stationery for my résumé?"

With nearly $50,000 in student loan debt, I made the heart-wrenching decision to sell my condo and move in with my mother, who was then living in a two-bedroom house in Palmdale, California. She was now in her fifties, and it was the first time she'd ever had a home of her own and one of the few times she'd ever lived alone, without my grandmother. I was proud of her. I thought I might take refuge there, with Mom, and catch my breath. Instead, it wasn't long before I discovered that I'd placed myself squarely in the eye of the storm.

The Mojave Desert was *Terminator* terrain, where filmmakers had shot the original film. From the window of Mom's upstairs bedroom, row upon row of Joshua trees stretched ahead—nothing but blond hills and rolling shrubbery. In the desert, I found a cleansing, scorching kind of stillness. The scenery was apt.

While jogging outside one morning, I stumbled upon some disturbing items clustered together along the side of the road. There were a crushed Marlboro box, a used condom, a broken beer bottle, and a torn blouse and panties. For a long time, I stood there dumbfounded. It was impossible to overlook the violent scene that played out in my mind. I saw terror, betrayal, and a woman broken. Suddenly, my body folded into itself. I crumbled onto the curbside and howled with rage. There were no people or cars. Just me. Alone and devastated, on a deserted road. Members of twelve-steps programs often refer to rock bottom as the point when you can finally begin again.

Was this mine?

Back home, Mom wanted to take medication for her long-standing depression and sadness. I thought she should first try exercising and changing her diet. We argued as if we were lawyers on opposing sides in a courtroom. All day, every day, she drank enormous tumblers of iced tea and then wondered why she couldn't sleep at night. Why not cut out the caffeine and sugar? I insisted. Why jump straight to drugs?

It began to dawn on me that our roles had always been reversed. For most of my life, I had been the one having to parent my mother. Now, when I desperately needed nurturing myself, the pattern continued, intensifying my pain. I remembered Michele's diagnosis, an imbalance of yin and yang. If my grandmother had fought too much in her life, my mother had not fought enough. Now, we were, all of us, at a crossroads. The choice was simple: We could continue as always. Or we could heal together.

I spoke to Jaime, my college boyfriend, for the first time in years. Now an Episcopalian priest with a small church in Hollywood, he was married to a biracial Black woman. After we spoke, he sent me a sermon he'd written. It was inspired by his son, he said, who was learning about butterflies in school. Tears cascaded down my cheeks as I read his words, which came to me at exactly the right time:

> How ironic that the cocoon has come to mean exactly the opposite of what it means to a caterpillar. A cocoon isn't safe. A cocoon is where a caterpillar risks it all, where it enters total chaos. Where it undergoes total rebuilding. Where it dies to one way of locomotion and is born to a new way of living. A cocoon is where a caterpillar allows itself to disintegrate so that it can emerge anew with sharpened sensory perceptions.

I dreamed of ghostlike children who crashed through the walls of my mother's home, their transparent bodies shaking the rooms so forcefully that the earth rumbled and groaned beneath them. I understood that the foundation of my life was being uprooted, demolished from within. The message of the dream was clear. My ghost children were clearing the way for new construction. They would destroy the old home and replace it with a dwelling place beyond anything I'd ever known. A home that would be solid enough to speak to new possibilities—new futures that I could not yet even begin to imagine.

hiding

A local California state college offered me a tenure-track job in Pan-African studies. The field wasn't really my thing, but I accepted anyway, abandoning my writing for a steady paycheck and health insurance. Teaching would allow me to get some treatment for my back pain, I reasoned. Maybe even a few sessions with a good psychologist.

At my first appointment with Judy, my new therapist, I opened my mouth to speak and didn't close it again for an hour. I told her about the heavy burden of my debt and being a struggling writer. I told her about the man who had molested me as a child, and about my mother's depression and the sadness that had spilled from her life into my own. I told her about how I had looked for my father but that finding him hadn't filled the hole inside. I told her about the back pain I had endured for years and how I'd seen a chiropractor and orthopedic surgeons and all they wanted to do was give me drugs and a new pillow, and nothing helped.

How amazing it was to lay all this out in simple sentences and have someone listen without judgment. Judy repeated my thoughts back to me, summarizing. As she did, the chaos of my mind slowed and halted in the quiet room.

"So . . ." She exhaled. "Why have you decided to come to therapy *now?*"

I shook my head, searching the walls. "I've just been working so hard . . . trying to prove myself."

"What are you trying to prove?"

We studied one another. "I just feel like I'm never good enough."

"Good enough for what?"

"I don't know."

Judy glanced at her hands, waiting.

"Love?"

She nodded, giving me space to continue.

Suddenly sobs lurched out of me, convulsing my body. "I can't do this anymore! I'm exhausted!"

She passed me a box of tissues and then waited some more. When she spoke again, her response was five simple words. Five words that set me aright for the first time in years.

"You have reason to be."

You have reason to be.

Judy began the arduous process of leading me out of a desert that was now both literal and figurative. During our sessions, I learned that daughters of absent fathers often idealize these shadow figures, holding them up as perfect in their fantasies. As adults, we may also choose lovers who are absent emotionally or physically and idealize those relationships too. The description fit. Aside from two meaningful long-term relationships, I had often gravitated toward men who offered nothing in the way of substance or stability.

My healing process continued, taking on various shapes and forms over the next several months. During this period, I was aware that nothing happened that wasn't of my own free will. "I create my own destiny" was a phrase I often repeated to myself. But it was also true that I sensed the clear presence of divine intervention at key points along the way. Yes, I had to want to heal, of my own free will. But once I made that choice, I believe that divinity showed up at every turn, helping to guide me. In addition to my therapist, Judy, a godsend if there ever was one, I had another guiding light.

Ginny was an intuitive life coach that I had worked with off and on for nearly a decade. Whenever I lost my way or felt stuck, she'd steered me back on track. Now, she was on the phone, repeating a question she had often put to me.

"Kristal, when are you going to stop hiding from your own life?"

I had no idea what she meant.

"Yes, you do," she insisted. "You've forgotten, again, who you are."

I wasn't anyone, I thought to myself. I was a failure.

"Well . . ." I answered. "I'm trying to get out of debt here."

She sighed. "Have you seen Oprah's new magazine?"

"You don't understand, Ginny. I have no time for that. I have classes to prepare."

She softened then, as though speaking to a child. "Kristal. Teaching is wonderful for those who have that calling. But it's thirty students in a classroom. You always wanted to be a voice in the *world*. Isn't that right? Isn't it the world you're concerned about?"

"Yes."

"So. Who do you know back east?"

"A lot of people, I guess."

"Well, why is it that you never speak to any of them?"

She was right about that. Being a professional loner was my modus operandi.

She was silent for a moment, tuning in.

"It's like their phone numbers are scattered around in a drawer."

My jaw dropped. Ginny lived in another state. She'd never been to my home. There was no way she could have known that. As it happened, I'd once had one of those old-fashioned wheel Rolodexes on my desk, but for some reason, I had decided some months or years earlier to pull out several of the cards that I thought worth keeping. I threw the rest of the wheel away—contacts and all—and tossed the remaining cards in a drawer, where they remained scattered and unorganized.

"Most of those people wouldn't even remember me," I countered.

"That's not true." She paused, sighing. "And anyway, you just have to take that leap of faith."

A chill shot through me. She had spoken the exact same words I had heard at the acupuncturist's office, the voice from my ear-touching vision.

The next day, I took Ginny's advice and called an editor acquaintance at the *Washington Post* whom I hadn't spoken to in years. Three weeks later, I found myself in Washington, DC, inside one of the paper's conference rooms, meeting with editors from the Arts & Style section.

Eugene Robinson shook my hand. "I love the clips you sent. Especially the Jamie Foxx cover for *Vibe*." They broke the news to me that there were no official staff openings in the Style section right now. "But let's see what we can work out," added Gene. Later, over lunch, I presented a detailed list of nine story ideas to Gene and an editor named John Pancake. Yes, yes, and yes, they said, ticking off each one in turn. They liked all of my ideas and could see them working well in the section. I had taken a complete leap of faith and it had worked. The next thing I knew, I was handing in my notice at my teaching job. I knew beyond a doubt that I would not have been in that position without divine guidance. *Show me. Lead me. Guide me. Thank you.*

"You were almost born in the East," Mom announced casually as I was packing suitcases, preparing to drive cross-country to my new apartment in Washington, DC.

"What?"

"Phil and I were supposed to travel all the way across the country. We went to Vegas for a while, and then to Phoenix. We were supposed to go to New Orleans next. I'm sure we would have made it to New York, eventually. You might have been born there if I hadn't decided to go back home."

It was a rare, open moment between us. I sat down on the bed next to her. "Why did you decide to go back?"

"I was scared. I told Phil that now that I was pregnant, I needed to find a doctor and have regular checkups. And I needed to be near my mother."

"What did he say?"

"He dropped me off at Dra's and went to New Orleans alone. That was the end of our cross-country adventure."

It was uncanny. Once I made the decision to move east, everything fit into place perfectly. Even my belongings—three suitcases of clothes, a small dresser, and a file cabinet of papers—slotted together like a precise Rubik's Cube into the trunk of my Jeep Cherokee. The ease of my relocation was unnerving. I attributed this to the fact that I was exactly where I belonged in that moment, no longer fighting with myself but, instead, following my heart.

I drove alone, with Caroline Myss's *Anatomy of the Spirit* as company, relishing the opportunity to stretch out across the open road. Setting out at sunrise each morning, I crossed Arizona, New Mexico, Texas, Oklahoma, Missouri, Illinois, Indiana, Ohio, and West Virginia at a leisurely pace, visualizing my life as it could be. I was at one with the mostly empty roads, in communion with the early morning long-haul truck drivers. Just before sundown, I stopped at whatever Courtyard or Hampton Inn was near and relaxed in the Jacuzzi before turning in early. As I neared the end of my journey, somewhere near Pennsylvania, I think, I pulled over to marvel at a blazing orange sunset and gave thanks for such an adventure.

And Ginny was right about another thing. Once I got to the East Coast, *O: The Oprah Magazine* did, in fact, buy one of my essays.

So, there was that too.

In the early 2000s, I was having the time of my life—living in New York City by then and writing for a host of newspapers and magazines while teaching part time at Columbia University's Graduate School of Journalism. There were drinks at Balthazar and dinners at Pastis with a trio of my closest girlfriends. Tatsha, Kemba, Carol, and I were all journalists, and we made a habit of brunching together—long Sundays with mimosas flowing well into the afternoon. Kind of like *Sex and the City* but for Black girls, as we sometimes liked to joke.

The *New York Times Sunday Magazine* had assigned another essay, and *Essence* made me a contributing writer. I had friends on Wall Street and at the Grammys and even a cool dude from the NBA. At thirty-seven, I rented a sixth-floor walk-up penthouse at Ninety-Fourth and Amsterdam whose crowning glory was a roof space to myself. I grew fresh eggplant and tomatoes outside a sliding glass door and threw the largest birthday party of my life under the stars.

I was moving and shaking and, to the outside world, doing just fine. But that's the thing about wounds of the soul. Only we know when they are still bleeding inside and when they are not. If someone goes in and starts digging and scratching, they can just as suddenly be ripped open again, exposed and stinging with pain.

My phone rang late one night. I reached for it groggily from bed and was surprised to hear my father's voice on the other end. "I just wanted to let you know that Michele died a few hours ago," he said.

"Oh. I'm so sorry to hear that."

"Yeah. You know she's had bladder cancer for the past six months."

"No, I didn't know that."

"Her body just finally gave up. She was only sixty-one."

"That's awful."

"You know, we were married for thirty-three years."

"I'm so sorry. You must be devastated."

Then my father said something that tore into the fragile space between us. "I talked to her by her bedside, you know, just before she died."

"Oh?"

"She told me to take care of you."

Stabbing pain shot through me.

"What?"

Michele had never wanted me in my father's life. In fact, she had actively discouraged it.

"Yeah. Just before she died, she said, 'Take care of Kristal.'"

"Oh. OK."

I'm sure my tone registered disbelief. It probably also fell short in the area of compassion. I don't exactly remember what I said next, but my reaction was no doubt less sympathetic than it should have been. The call ended on an awkward note, and I hung up the phone with an overpowering sense of rage. *Why say such a thing to me now?* I thought. *Why not do it when you had the chance? Where were you when I needed you? Where were you when I was a child who needed her father?* I shut down, refusing to grieve for the woman who had done me such irreparable harm. Take care of me now? When I was a grown-ass woman having the time of my life in New York City? Oh, hell no.

Over the years, I had taken countless leaps of faith for the sake of my relationship with my father. Again and again, I had given him every opportunity to come correct. Now, I made a fateful decision. Just like that, I was done. I would not give him, or our relationship, another ounce of energy.

What I didn't realize when I made this silent pronouncement was that there is no "in-between" in healing. It's an all-or-nothing proposition. You either do it or you don't. Forgive, or stay stuck.

Not long afterward, a friend gave me a book of visualization exercises. Flipping through the pages I found one called "The Three." *Why not?* I thought one day, stretching out on my yoga mat and closing my eyes. It couldn't hurt. Toni Cade Bambara once said that everything we needed was already here—all the information, teachers, and resources. "You simply have to know how to be still and receive," she said. So I decided to try.

Imagine walking along the beach. Breathe. Hear the waves. Relax. Now, just ahead, notice three figures gathered around a fire. They are your heart, mind, and spirit. Ask them what you need to know.

It was a little wacky, I had to admit. But I figured stranger things had been known to work. To my surprise, my own personal three figures revealed themselves immediately. The man was aggressive. I called him Lionel, like a lion. He was my mind. Draping a slick arm around my shoulders, he steered me away from the fire, plotting as if we were cooking up a small-town hustle. "Whatever you need. Just let me know."

"Wait!" I held back as he tried to lead me away. "I need to meet all three of you."

He scrunched his face. "Aw, man! You know them. They're wimps! Come on! We don't need them!"

But I insisted, returning to the campfire, where I found a Violet, a child, shivering and crying in the sand. She was my heart.

Marta, my spirit, sat silently at her side.

I repeated this unconventional exercise over the next several days and each time, Lionel insisted on doing things his way. He was exhausting. I had to work just to convince him even to *look* at the girl. Then, one day, I'd had enough. Outside I was calm, meditating on my yoga mat, but inside something detonated with rage. "You think you're so smart, Lionel! But the only reason you're here is because *she's* been carrying you," I said, pointing to Violet. "*She* endures all your ridiculous plans! *She* suffers the consequences! She suffers because of *you*. You're nothing without her!"

That's when my experiment got interesting.

The next time I returned to the campfire scene, what I saw amazed me. Lionel cradled the girl in his arms, his coat draped across her body for warmth. He stroked her hair and comforted her. This new scene repeated itself for some time until, one day, Lionel burst into tears. I understood his emotion as a profound breakthrough. Then I watched the scene, stunned, as Marta spoke for the first time. "I don't want your guilt." She fixed her gaze on Lionel. "I want your humility. Understand that you don't know all. Can't fix all. We are here too. We matter."

For several weeks, I returned to the three figures, observing and listening. Now, Lionel fed Violet roasted meat from the fire, smiling shyly. There was a new humility to him. Gradually, Violet came out of her shell, becoming chatty and confident. "He's taking me fishing today!" she sang out one morning before splashing into the ocean. I took the hint. Easing out of my meditation, I made my way to the grocery store for fresh salmon.

Another morning Marta met me on the sand. We sat side by side for a time, watching the waves foam. Then she turned to face me.

"I need something from you."

"Oh?" She rarely spoke, so I knew that whatever it was, it must be important. "What?"

"Time." She held my gaze for a moment before returning her attention to the crashing waves.

What an interesting notion, I thought, unfolding my yoga legs and coming back into my day.

My spirit wants more time with me.

an adventure

If I had learned anything during my dark hour of the soul, it was that divine guidance must be followed, regardless of whether or not the instruction seems to make sense at the time. I valued what Marta had told me and determined that I would indeed find a way to spend some time with my soul.

Taking my place on a six-seat commuter plane from Fort Lauderdale, I was headed to the island of Bimini, where I would board a fifty-foot trimaran and embark on a seven-day journey to swim with wild dolphins, something I had always wanted to do. The trip reminded me of my younger, more adventurous self—the one who jetted off alone to see the tropical rainforest of El Yunque and the ancient ruins at Caguana in Puerto Rico. That was the Kristal who, inspired by June Jordan's *Living Room*, volunteered to travel to Nicaragua and offer her Spanish translation services in the midst of a civil war. The Kristal who had spent her junior year of college studying abroad in Madrid, Spain. The same Kristal who had enrolled in a grueling graduate school program, far from the familiarity of home. *That* Kristal.

After boarding the boat, however, I couldn't help wondering if I'd made a mistake. To start, the captain, whom I'll call Bill, didn't allow us to wear shoes, which meant that I was constantly wiping dirt, dead mosquito wings, and dog hair from the bottoms of my feet. *Disgusting.* Second, although I'd paid extra for a private bathroom, the toilet and sink in my bunk were broken, which meant that I would have to share with my cabinmates. And no, I would not receive a refund for the inconvenience. (Bill pointed to the "no refund" clause in the contract.)

Dinnertime brought fresh disappointment as I discovered that the boat's so-called all-inclusive meals were frighteningly frugal. In fact, our first dinner consisted of nothing more than a lettuce and tomato "wrap." "Chef" Amy, the captain's girlfriend, even had the nerve to place gratuity envelopes beside our plates.

I tried to put these complaints aside. Dra and Mom had taught us that everything in life happened for a reason, and I firmly believed in that maxim. When you don't know why you've arrived somewhere or what the ultimate purpose is, it was best to settle into the knowledge that a higher authority was at work, and for a higher good, whether you grasped its meaning or not. God had brought me to this place. The best thing to do now, I decided, was to allow unseen forces to simply unfold.

On day one, Captain Bill went over some ground rules.

"We might never see a single dolphin," he warned, again pointing to the contract. "Whatever happens out there is entirely up to the animals." Actually, it was the rule I liked most about the entire operation. Petting a captive animal at a water park just wasn't something I wanted to support. "If they decide to join us," Bill continued, "remember that there is to be no touching, no feeding, and no chasing. These are wild creatures. Allow them to come to you if, and when, they choose to do so." *Amen and amen*, as my grandmother liked to say.

The next morning, we anchored at what Bill thought to be a good location, buckled up our diving gear and oxygen, and prepared to slide into the warm Caribbean waters. I had befriended two cabinmates: Maria, a retired flight attendant, and Simone, a yoga instructor. We exchanged nervous glances as we sank into the abyss of the Gulf Stream. *Was this really a good idea?* I thought, hesitating. It was unsettling not being able to breathe from the nose. I began to panic. This was not smart. The skills needed for this were well above my amateur snorkeling training. And was I hyperventilating?

I heard Bill's garbled voice from a faraway place above the surface. "Learning to breathe from the mouth requires trust. Just remember that you did it in the womb." I tried to calm my inhalations. "It's all about surrender," Bill droned on. "You have to be willing to sink down into the darkness and know that you will not drown." But did I know that? I wasn't so sure.

Day two was an improvement. Steeling myself, I plunged right in and was rewarded with a dazzling discovery. Just beneath the surface lay a mind-boggling alternate universe. Hundreds of striped sergeant majors darted under my arms and between my legs. Bug-eyed squirrelfish hid in coral recesses, and beige flounder hovered invisibly over the sandy ocean floor, their camouflaged color a perfect match for their environment. Then came my favorites: the rainbow parrotfish. I couldn't help smiling at their bright orange heads and comical turquoise lips as they slipped past me.

And just like that, there was magic: dozens of dolphins.

Simone, Maria, and I bobbed on the surface as they surrounded us. We grinned at them, and at one another. Dolphins, I had read, were highly evolved, intelligent creatures. Unlike other mammals, they did not dream but instead remained aware of every breath, even while sleeping—which had made them the perfect source for a study on REM sleep at UCLA. In other words, as one researcher put it, there was no such thing as an unconscious dolphin.

They stayed for hours, frolicking and playing in the sun. At some point, I hoisted myself back onto the boat and lay face down on the net, peering into the water below. Dolphins pranced remarkably close to my face. A smooth, gray bottlenose parked herself so close to me that I was able to make a study of her fin, which had a large, downward-curved scratch at the bottom and five lighter-colored lines. "Is that five scratches or six?" I said aloud for no particular reason. "Show me your fin again so I can count." To my astonishment she swam closer, as if she had understood every word, and poked her fin out of the water.

Elated, I ran to the rear of the boat, geared up, and hoisted myself back into the water. My dolphin friend followed, swimming around the side of the boat to join me. Ducking underwater, I studied her again. Yes, it was her. One long scratch and five lighter ones. Until that moment my underwater breathing had been slightly frantic. Now, in the dolphin's presence, it somehow slowed.

Then she did something absolutely remarkable that, to this day, I have not been able to explain or even to fully understand. She swam a perfect circle around my body and paused directly in front of me, vertical and upright, as if asking a question. Next, she circled my body again, this time in the opposite direction, pausing again in an upright position to question me. Maria and Simone watched the entire exchange and were as dumbfounded by it as I was.

In one of the many dolphin books I'd brought onboard, I read that they often circled protectively around the weakest members of the group. So, was that it? Of the eight or nine people onboard, was I the one most in need of protection?

"That happened once before," Bill told us later that night over a dinner of beans and rice. "There was a woman who came from Texas," he said, "and a dolphin singled her out, bumping her like this." He poked a finger at his chest. "Tap, tap, tap. When she got home, her doctor told her that she had breast cancer in the exact same spot the dolphin had been nudging."

The next morning, a few of us gathered on deck for a sunrise yoga session with Simone. "Think of an intention and repeat it to yourself silently three times," she instructed. You would have thought she'd asked me to calculate advanced physics. My brain went into overdrive, thrashing this way and that. I wanted to run, to flee. What was happening? I forced myself to breathe until, somewhere in the chaos, I managed to complete a thought.

I want love. Later, Simone and I took a walk along the shoreline, brown-sugar sand between our toes. Wading in the warm water, we shared snippets of our life stories. Like me, she had never known her father. And like me, she, too, was sexually assaulted by a neighbor as a child. Her trauma was repeated later, by her mother's boyfriend. We fell silent after our mutual confessions. It had rained earlier in the day and a smoky indigo sky bled into gray clouds.

Simone turned to face me.

"You know what's strange?"

I shook my head.

"I've been happily married for twenty-five years. We have three grown children." She shook her head. "But, to this day, there's a part of me that is still waiting for my husband to abandon me."

I realized then that it was no accident that I had chosen this boat, at this particular time in my life. Nor was it an accident that I'd been given the book of visualizations, or that Marta had led me to this moment and to this very conversation.

The next time we gathered on deck for yoga, Simone repeated the same instruction: "Think of an intention and repeat it three times in your mind. Know that whatever it is, this intention has already come into being." This time, to my amazement, my brain offered no resistance. *I want love. I want love. I want love*, I repeated. *I intend to love. I intend to be loved.*

At the Bimini Museum, there is a photograph of Ernest Hemingway displaying a captured fifty-pound marlin. The novelist apparently spent seven hours battling the fish, according to the museum's curator, losing a pound in sweat for every hour of the fight. Afterward, he got drunk on rum and used the marlin as a punching bag. As I listened to this story, I thought of my mother and grandmother fighting; sometimes too much and other times, perhaps not enough. They knew how to fight the world but never quite mastered the art of fighting for their own well-being or their own internal harmony. They never quite cleansed themselves of old guilts, judgments, and resentments.

It occurred to me that we all beat the wrong fish, at times, just like Hemingway, who had been one of my favorite authors in college. We all replayed patterns of behavior, unsure of how to escape the loop. I knew now that not everything in life was meant to be a battle. But did it follow that the answer to every conflict was surrender? And what was one to do when surrender felt like death by drowning?

My father and I were mostly communicating by email then, our exchanges less and less fulfilling. As I approached my fortieth birthday, I realized that my fight with him was over. I would not wrestle with that dead fish anymore, or continue to beat his carcass. My father must have felt the shift too. His last message to me was a quick note, just to let me know that an earthquake had hit Vashon and that it had "engulfed his spirit with a veil of wonder and awe." His reverent musings were typical, but when I glanced at the signature, I found something completely unexpected. He had signed off in a way I'd never seen before.

"Love, Phil."

Not Dad. *Phil.*

It had been two decades since I first found my father, tracking him down and engineering a relationship out of fantasies and thin air. But now, to even my own astonishment, I was about to give him up again. Trusting Violet, my now-thriving heart, it felt healthier to me somehow to simply stand alone, rather than to continue waiting for something that would not come.

My father didn't press the matter. He simply let me go.

alfonso

I was invited to Dallas, Texas, to give a speech about my new book, *Black Women's Lives: Stories of Power and Pain*. The same pages that an editor had rejected a decade earlier now had a home with Nation Books, a smaller, supportive press. I delighted in these talks, using them as a chance to honor the women profiled in the book. There were a Mississippi catfish plant worker, an organic dairy farmer in Vermont, a California filmmaker, a CEO in New York, an environmental justice activist in Alabama, and a Georgia elementary school principal, among others. Standing at a podium in an auditorium at El Centro College, I launched into a familiar talk that I'd already given at a dozen other bookstores and universities. This time, though, something was different. Or maybe it was I who was different.

As I connected the dots between the stories in the book, I could feel the audience moving with me, feeling the same pangs of joy and anxiety that I had felt throughout my writing journey. Wrapping up, I smiled and thanked them. Then, to my utter astonishment, something amazing happened. I watched in disbelief as the audience of more than two hundred faculty, students, and staff rose from their chairs, applauding in scattered bursts that grew progressively louder. It was my first standing ovation. *Ever*. Even in the years since that day, I would give dozens of talks, but never again would I receive a reception quite like that one. Why? I can't be sure. But there was something in the air. Something about that day was special.

I arrived at Dallas Fort Worth International Airport giddy with confidence. Somehow, against all odds, I had finally become the voice that I'd always dreamed of being. This was it. *This* was my moment. I knew, also, that whatever transformation I'd undergone over the years leading to this moment had come from the inside out. I had taken my demons on and fought the good fight. Whatever good fortune was now manifesting in my life could not have come, I believed, if I had not done the work of healing myself from within.

The truth was, at forty, I was no longer the lost and confused young woman I'd once been. Prayer, counsel, and faith had strengthened me. My dreams were proof of the profound shifts that had taken place. Gone were the bathroom nightmares that I'd battled in my twenties and thirties. Gone were the panicked images of flight and rape. In their place, I now dreamed constantly of water, strangely. There were oceans, lakes, creeks, and cascading waterfalls everywhere—even bathtubs and rain puddles.

Another image that showed up regularly in my nighttime consciousness was odd but fitting. I dreamed of the produce sections of grocery stores, where I saw myself regularly shopping for green things: kale, cucumber, bell peppers, Granny Smith apples, spinach, celery. Cleansing things. Clearly, a deeper part of myself was hard at work as I slept, showing me exactly what to do and how to do it.

Physically, too, I was different. For one thing, I hadn't touched caffeine in years. Also, these days, I sat down to write only after a good night's rest and a hearty breakfast. No more skipping meals. I had filled out slightly in my hips and legs, which was a good thing. The extra five or ten pounds softened the hard edges, evidence that I was kinder and gentler to my body.

At the airport, the good omens kept coming. I snagged a seat on an earlier flight at the last minute, putting me back in New York at a reasonable hour of the night. What a blessing this day has been, I thought to myself, smiling as I tugged my rolling suitcase down the aisle toward my seat.

"Can I help you with your bag?" A handsome stranger wearing a suit and tie looked up from his seat. He had dark hair and eyes. A foreign accent.

"Yes, thank you!" I may have been a feminist, but with my aching back, every extra muscle was a godsend. As he hoisted my suitcase into the overhead bin, I stole another glance at my ticket. This was the place: 10A. We exchanged polite smiles and I settled into the window seat beside him.

Once we were in the air, I cracked open my book and was about to enjoy a celebratory glass of wine when Alfonso struck up a conversation.

"What are you reading?"

"Oh. A biography about Spinoza." It sounded much loftier than it was. I picked up the book only because I remembered something Zora Neale Hurston had once said that had piqued my interest: that, one day, she hoped to "reread Spinoza" in a leisurely way.

Alfonso nodded.

"Are you visiting New York, or going home?" I asked. The question was preventative. After Damien, my Australian boyfriend, I'd had my fill of long-distance relationships.

"Home." He smiled slightly. "You?"

"Home, too." Smile.

He blinked, but only a little, and only with his left eye—his lashes sweeping down as if in slow motion. It was an odd, unconscious mannerism that I found both endearing and sexy. As we chatted, I learned that Alfonso, an international corporate tax attorney, had also been scheduled to take a different plane to New York that day. He'd run late after his conference and had missed the earlier flight. Like me, he'd changed his ticket at the last minute, and now, here we were: seated side by side on American Airlines flight 748. Do soulmates appear only when we are ready for them? Or do we make ourselves ready, so that soulmates can finally appear?

Originally from Madrid, Spain, Alfonso was now living in New York for the second time, after attending Columbia University Law School as an exchange student some years earlier. We also discovered that during my own year studying abroad in Madrid as a junior in college, I'd lived in the same neighborhood where he grew up. We might have passed each other on the streets of Moncloa. Perhaps he'd shot past me on his Vespa while cruising the Avenida Reina Victoria. Or maybe I'd bought bread in the same bakery where his mother shopped.

"Do you have children?" I saw that he wore no wedding band.

"I have a daughter, Maria. She's five."

He told me that he was separated from his wife but that he went back to Spain once a month to see Maria. Looking back on the conversation, I would often wonder if that was the moment when I fell for him. Unlike my own father, Alfonso had gone back for his daughter again and again and again. I could see by the way he spoke of her that he would never stop going back for Maria.

Between the silences, we peered out at a distant lightning storm behind gray-pink clouds. When we landed, we shared a cab to the city—something neither of us had ever done with anyone. Outside my Harlem apartment, I reached into my purse for a business card and handed it to him.

Alfonso studied it for a moment, hesitating. "Do you really want me to call?"

I grinned. Somehow, he was both manly and innocent at once.

"Yes. I really want you to call."

So many of the men I had dated before had been self-involved and emotionally unavailable. Alfonso was different. With him, there were none of the usual cat-and-mouse games. Not once did he leave me to wonder where he stood or what he was feeling. "It has barely been an hour since I left you and already, I can't wait to see you again," he emailed after our first date. Alfonso fascinated me. He was not the least bit afraid of his own vulnerability.

We jogged around the Central Park Reservoir late one afternoon and met for dinner and margaritas at Canyon Road. We took long, late-night walks across the city, pausing at stoplights for lingering kisses. When I mentioned that I loved Spanish tortillas, Alfonso called his mother for the recipe and made one for the first time, with sweet, cooked onions. Before long, he announced that he was falling in love with me. His gaze was unguarded. I had never seen such openness in a man.

In past relationships, I had always cultivated my mother's cool reserve. The women in my family operated this way on autopilot. I thought that I was unassailable, with my walls and protective barriers. It wasn't until Alfonso came along that I realized there could be another way. Through his example, I began to see that only the truly strong among us were courageous enough to risk their hearts. He came at precisely the right time. He came when I had grown weary of steeliness.

"What's wrong?" Alfonso asked one morning as he was heading out the door. We were living together in a one-bedroom apartment on Forty-Fourth and Lexington near Grand Central Station.

"Nothing."

"No. Tell me."

It made no difference that he was dressed, with a suitcase ready at the door. No difference that his flight would be boarding soon. Alfonso stopped everything. "I'm not leaving until you tell me." Setting his briefcase on the counter, he moved us to the couch to sit down.

"What's wrong?"

"I don't know."

Truly, I didn't. It was a vague, nagging feeling. Probably something about hotels and the possibility of infidelity. But with Alfonso's gentle prodding, whatever insecurity I might have been entertaining welled up to the surface in such a rush that it surprised even me. Out came the buried fears, spilling into the light of his embrace. It amazed me how the monsters of my imagination became small once exposed and acknowledged. Bit by bit, he chipped away at my walls, teaching me that it was human to be sad, or worried, or vulnerable. Emotions weren't the enemy, and it wasn't my lifelong job to constantly hide or conquer them.

Not long after we met, I was scheduled to have surgery for fibroids during the holiday season. Mom flew to New York, ostensibly to help me through the operation. But it didn't quite work out that way. Instead, it was Alfonso who went with me to the pre-op doctor's appointments. It was Alfonso who slept by my side at the hospital and cooked meals for me to have ready post-surgery.

Time and again, his nurturing spoke to the little girl in me, offering her the attention she craved. He even bought me a Christmas teddy bear from the hospital gift shop, which I clung to with a surprising ferocity as I lay writhing in pain. I wanted to be rocked and comforted. Strange as it may have seemed, I wanted to be mothered.

In contrast, Mom's behavior was suddenly jarring as I watched her responses to me through the eyes of an outsider. I could see Alfonso's shock as she rushed off to her hotel room for a bath rather than staying with me in the hospital. Or as she wondered aloud where she might go in Harlem to get her hair braided after my surgery. Alfonso would be leaving for Spain soon, to spend Christmas with his daughter. If Mom were to follow through on her planned four- or five-hour hair expedition, there would be no one at home even to help me limp from the bed to the bathroom. For the first time in my life, I was embarrassed by her lack of tenderness. But my mother hadn't changed. She was simply following our family motto, which said we all had our own burdens to carry. We all had to learn how to soldier on, alone. From her point of view, it must have seemed as though *I* were the one suddenly defecting from that army.

Summers, Alfonso and I vacationed with his family in Almería, a small town at the southeastern tip of the Iberian Peninsula. His parents kept an apartment in Aguadulce, our corner of the beach, where there were a few German tourists, perhaps, but no Americans.

On our first trip there, I could still toss Maria, giggling, across the pool. Now, four years later, she was a tween. Unloading a boogie board at the beach, she stretched out on the sand and called up videos of Selena Gomez on an iPhone. Before meeting Alfonso, I hadn't spent much time with children. The truth was, I wasn't even sure I knew how. Playing with Maria and her cousins sparked something in me that I hadn't quite known was there. I began to see myself as someone who might make a good mother. Now in my early forties, I knew that my chances of getting pregnant were slim. Still, I told myself that anything was possible. Alfonso and his family inspired me to imagine a family in a way I'd never allowed myself to do before. What's more, I now had a strong inner compass that I had grown accustomed to trusting. When I saw Violet in my visualizations these days, she was a grown woman who knew exactly what she wanted. The three figures had relocated from the beach, and now,

Violet was mistress of her own domain: a plush green garden, where she tended to her flowers wearing flowing white linen. When I listened to what she had to say, my heart's desire shone with unmistakable clarity. There was no question about it.

Violet wanted to be a mother.

After swimming and sunning ourselves at the beach at Almería, we shuffled with Alfonso's large clan to an outdoor table at El Palmeral restaurant. Plopping down in our swimsuits, we greeted familiar waiters who cracked off-color Spanish jokes as they laid out blanched almonds and green olives. The smell of monkfish grilled in garlic wafted toward us from the kitchen. Sipping a cold beer, I surveyed the large table. Alfonso's parents were there, Paquita and Jose, along with two of his sisters and their combined pack of children. I laughed as the family talked over one another, all at once, which made it nearly impossible for me to follow the conversation.

That's when it hit me. In a flash, a realization so new and unusual crashed into me so hard that it nearly bowled me over. So this is what it feels like, I thought, to be a part of a family with no one missing. *Men, as well as women. Boys, as well as girls.* Alfonso's father, Jose, always took special delight in pouring my wine first for sampling. "Toma, hija," he said, passing a new red to me and waiting for my reaction. Tears welled in my eyes. *A father and a grandfather.*

Seven years had passed since I had spoken with my own father. When Alfonso and I began to make wedding plans that summer, I decided that it wasn't possible for me to embark on something as important as marriage while still harboring old resentments. Although I'd come a long way in my efforts to sweep away the dustbins of hurt and shame from my past, I realized that healing was a long and often nonlinear process, complete with setbacks and dead ends.

I wasn't done yet.

So once again, I reached out to my father.

It was the middle of the night. Everyone was asleep as I powered up my laptop computer. "I need to forgive you," I wrote in an email, "but I'm not sure how." I poured my emotions onto the page in a flurry of pent-up emotion and unresolved grief:

I know that I need to open my heart and allow it to happen. The past is done and gone for both of us. I forgive you, for the father you never were, and for the father you tried to be. I forgive you. Thank you for playing a part in bringing me into this glorious world. Thank you for this life. I forgive you. Go in peace.

I hit "send" but my message bounced back. "Undeliverable."

a new life

My grandmother was playing solitaire and watching television when I called. She was ninety now, with early-stage Alzheimer's disease.

"Is it cold there?"

"Dra, you remember we moved to Miami, right?" Leaving New York City was the last thing I wanted to do, but relocating had meant a promotion for Alfonso and lower taxes for us both.

"Oh, yes, that's right."

"So, it's pretty warm almost all the time here."

"It must be nice to get away from the cold."

"It is."

I waited for Dra's standard speech. Because of her illness, she now had a habit of repeating three or four well-worn thoughts. "Well, I was just sitting here thinking to myself . . . we are so blessed, aren't we?"

I smiled. "Yes, we are."

"All of my children and grandchildren are healthy. No one is in jail." She chuckled slightly at this, as she always did. We all did, actually, every time she said it. As if so many of us had ever been to jail. Somehow, it was her way of assessing what might have been. "I don't have to go out trudging through the streets," she continued in an exaggerated voice, laughing, "trying to scrounge up bail money." Dra's repeated ruminations were funny, but they were also part of a larger shift. Somehow, over the years, her long-held belief in our generational family curse seemed to have dissipated. Just as my bathroom dreams had gradually disappeared, so too had Dra found a way to rewrite the narrative of her own life.

And she was right. We *were* blessed.

Some years earlier, I'd accepted a full-time position at Hofstra University on Long Island, teaching journalism while I continued to write articles and books. I'd climbed the ranks and was now a full professor with tenure (an honor that I later learned only about 30 percent of those with PhDs hold). In addition, I was director of our MA Journalism program, earning a solid salary. My job wouldn't be easy to replicate in Miami. And so, after much consideration, Alfonso and I decided that I would stay at Hofstra, commuting three days a week.

"Dra?"

"Mmmm?"

"What do you think your life would have been like if you hadn't had children?"

Because of her illness, I'd never wanted to burden Dra with my struggle to get pregnant. In fact, I was still smarting from Mom's reaction when I'd first raised the subject with her some years earlier. "I thought that train had left the station a long time ago," she blurted. Needless to say, I didn't bother looking for her emotional support again. But now, after two failed pregnancies, I was in desperate need of Dra's reassurance; the kind she had always provided on our Sunday afternoon phone calls.

Dra thought for a moment. "Well, I wouldn't really be living if I didn't have children. They're the blessing of my life."

Suddenly, tears cascaded down my cheeks.

"What do you think about me not having children?"

"But . . ." Her tone was incredulous, as if she couldn't understand why I would even ask such a thing. "You've traveled . . . and you've influenced people with your writing. You know, years ago, we couldn't even imagine getting on an airplane and sitting next to a white person." She searched her memory. "And don't you teach?"

"Yes."

"What is it . . . writing?"

"Yes."

"Well, see there! You have a career, and you impart that knowledge to young people."

"Yes. But it's just not the way I hoped things would be."

"Oh, sweetheart. Listen to me now. Don't you compare your life to *nobody's*, you hear me?" Just like that, miraculously, my grandmother was back. "God created you to serve *your* purpose in this world, and your purpose is not the same as anybody else's. Be grateful with what God has allowed you to accomplish."

For years, she had kept a photocopied paragraph on her bedroom dresser. It summed up her philosophy of life perfectly, in a nutshell:

> If you get up on the wrong side of the bed, it is no one's fault but your own. . . . Life is a challenge! African tradition tells us that it does not matter what difficulties we face. Our worth is measured by how we face those difficulties. If we are to grow and reach our fullest potential, we have no time to waste on bad days.

"You don't have *nothing* to cry about," Dra continued. "You hear?"

"Yes."

"Do you want me to pray with you before we hang up?"

"Um hm."

In Miami, Alfonso and I began to carve out a new life that moved at a pleasantly slow pace. The very thing I had dreaded losing—New York's frenetic energy—ironically became exactly that which I was happiest to leave behind. Life took its time in the humid air. We smiled more. There were Miami Heat games where we sat so close to the floor we could practically smell LeBron James's sweat. I joined a book club for the first time in my life—a group of smart, engaging women who quickly became some of my closest friends. Alfonso and I made annual trips to a couples-only resort in Ocho Rios, Jamaica. We took long, scenic drives to the Keys. And we also did something totally new that we'd never done before in ten years of dating and marriage: dancing for hours together to live bands at Blue Martini.

One evening, Alfonso took me for branzino at my favorite restaurant, Il Gabbiano, in Biscayne Bay. We nestled close on the waterfront terrace as a red sun sank into the horizon.

"What?" I asked. He'd worn a sly expression all afternoon. Something was up.

He smiled and ordered a bottle of Veuve Clicquot.

"Are we celebrating?"

"Yes."

Reaching into his pocket, he placed a small turquoise box into my hand. It was from Tiffany & Co., where we had bought our wedding rings.

I gasped. "What's this?"

That was his cue, I saw. He geared up to make what was clearly a prepared speech.

"In Spain, when a woman has a baby, it's customary for her husband to give her a ring." His eyes were tender. Careful. He took my hand. "You've tried harder than anyone in the world to be a mother. You've given your whole heart and body. And you're a wonderful stepmother to Maria. There is no one on earth who deserves this more than you."

The moment was somehow even more profound than his marriage proposal. I opened the box and found a sapphire-and-diamond-studded band, which instantly became more precious to me than anything else I had ever owned—even more than my wedding rings. This one was built on our shared hope and suffering, and on our resilience. This one cemented our bond. It also symbolized an ending and a resolution for us both, I realized. I had not been willing to admit defeat before, but now I could see that time had come. Our quest to have a baby had ended. It was time to surrender my heart's desire to God.

The pool cleaner's net made gentle splashing sounds as it filled with autumn leaves. It was late October, but the Florida heat was still scorching. We'd bought a house in Coconut Grove, a neighborhood thick with avocado, fig, mango, and, of course, coconut trees. I'd planted okra and tomatoes in our backyard, thrilled to be once again growing my own vegetables. Coco, our four-year-old cockapoo, slept beside my chair as I wrote from my home office, his body curled into a ball. Across the living room, I could hear Alfonso talking in loud, animated tones on a business call as he passed through the kitchen and back to our converted garage, which doubled as a man cave and second home office.

My cell phone rang, interrupting my train of thought. I wasn't particularly happy to see the name on the screen. It was the director of a disappointing adoption agency we'd hired a year earlier (our second). Both she and her staff were careless, sloppy, and dangerously deceptive. We hadn't entirely ruled out legal action.

"Lori, can you hold on?" I put the phone on mute and crossed to the front of the house, bringing Alfonso back to my office so we could take the call together.

"I have good news," she said, cutting to the chase. "A birth mother has chosen you." Alfonso and I stared at each other. Should we trust them? Was it a trick to get more money out of us? The agency was, indeed, full of trickery, and we were right not to trust them. Instead, we did something else. We trusted the birth mother, whom I'll call Melanie. Against the agency's wishes, I somehow found a way to communicate with her directly, and from that moment on, I knew we were on the right path. Alfonso and I learned that despite the agency's attempts to talk her out of choosing us (a longer story about greed and corruption in the adoption industry), Melanie had held fast. She knew what she knew. It had to be Alfonso and Kristal, she told them, and that was final.

Within weeks, we found ourselves in another state, in a hospital room, meeting Melanie. We were a match. There was no question about it for any of us. That night, Alfonso and I stretched out in a hospital room which had been set aside specifically for adoptive parents. We waited.

Then came our miracle.

The next morning, just after 8:30 a.m., a nurse placed our daughter, born minutes earlier, into our arms. I could not believe what I was seeing. She was perfect. Healthy. Beautiful. *Olivia.* She slept with us that first night in the hospital, and every night afterward. She breathed into my chest and made sweet gurgling sounds in my ear as I read to her from her very first book, *Safe and Snug*. We camped out in a local hotel waiting for interstate approval on the night of the 2016 presidential election, when I (mistakenly) announced to my baby girl that we were about to have the first woman president.

Two weeks later the paperwork was done. Alfonso loaded up a rented minivan with formula and diapers and drove us back to Florida. We arrived in Coconut Grove and placed our sleeping baby in her crib, below a framed image of a boy in the desert reading to a kneeling elephant, a symbol of hope that we had carted around from home to home for nearly ten years.

Our precious daughter was finally home.

Olivia was an outstanding eater who quickly doubled her weight. She had perfect little chubby cheeks, arms, and legs and enjoyed almost every food I fed her. (She would remain adventurous with food, happy to eat everything from artichoke hearts to octopus.) As a baby, she was quick to smile and laugh, with curly ringlets of dark hair and soulful, oval-shaped brown eyes. "What color am I?" she would ask me later, at four, as we read *Honeysmoke* together. "You're a beautiful brown girl," I would tell her. "African American and white, and Southeast Asian, with ancestry from a place called Laos."

I was an older mom, that was true. Every day I wrestled with that uncomfortable fact, hoping that Olivia would not come to resent my age. But with my years also came benefits. We were financially secure and stable in our relationship. My job at Hofstra even allowed me to take a partially paid sabbatical, which meant that I was able to stay home during Olivia's entire first year.

On Saturday mornings, I'd take her to Silly Monkeys Playhouse for the Music and Movement class, where she loved bobbing to Latin beats. In the evenings, I played old-school funk in the living room and we bounced around to throwbacks, such as the Brothers Johnson's "Strawberry Letter 23." At the Coconut Grove library, we sprawled out on the rug in the children's room, exploring picture books. Then, at home, after bath time, it was "two books" before bed, a tradition that continues to this day (although it's since been shortened to one book). My favorite part, though, was rocking her to sleep. I loved to feel her tiny cheek against my neck as we lulled ourselves with world music from Benin, Madagascar, South Africa, and Japan. I smelled and touched her constantly. I loved, loved, loved her. Alfonso and I both fell so deeply, deeply in love.

I would not want to romanticize motherhood, although it was, and is, impossibly romantic. During those early years, I was also constantly overwhelmed and more exhausted than I imagined possible. All of these emotions were present at the same time. Once, I remember feeling, literally, like such a walking zombie that I was unable to process the most basic thought. I remember staring into space, so sleep-deprived that I'd forgotten, or was unable, even to eat. Finally, I dragged myself to Subway and stared at passing cars blankly while I ingested a sandwich on autopilot.

And yet, motherhood had a magical, surreal quality. If I thought being Olivia's mom would become more ordinary with time, I was wrong. There was always something new to see and learn through her eyes. If I thought my emotions were in check and that I had become accustomed to holding my small, miraculous bundle, I was wrong again. My heart was now, and would always be, perpetually exposed. Perpetually vulnerable.

Once, when Olivia was a newborn, I burst into uncontrollable tears while reading her the book *You Are My I Love You* by Maryann Cusimano Love and Satomi Ichikawa. Pressing my baby close, I could scarcely see the words on the page through my joy. "I am your dandelion. You are my first wish."

"Olivia?" I whispered into her ear, but she was already sleeping.

"I am your finish line. You are my new path." I wept and wept and wept.

"I am your dinner. You are my chocolate cake."

multiracial

A demographic shift was sweeping the nation in the early 2000s, one that went beyond the outdated confines of Black and white that I had known growing up. Young people were now presenting themselves with new combinations of unexpected heritages. They were Punjabi and Guatemalan; Dominican and Nigerian; Peruvian and Thai. A quarter of a million mixed-race babies were being born each year, and my daughter was one of them. In Miami–Dade County alone, 34,000 people claimed two or more races.

I'd watched these young people over the years in my university classes and noticed that there was almost no societal understanding of what their experiences meant, both privately and to the culture at large. Instead, there were outdated patterns of perception and behavior that no one had bothered to update. Now, I saw that there was a new generation of multiracial youth who were living a different reality than the one I'd grown up with. They'd tired of explaining themselves to strangers and, unlike me, had not felt the burden of having to "prove" one's racial authenticity quite so acutely. These kids refused to be boxed in one way or another. Despite the pain of their outsider status, they saw themselves in a positive light, often, and as a bridge to the other side.

It made sense if you looked at it in context.

My great-grandfather was a white plantation owner in Arkansas. In the mid-1960s, at the time of my birth, we were, all of us, still too perilously close to our slave-slaveowner shared history to entertain premature notions of racial fluidity. You were either Black, or you weren't. Period. Pick a side. End of story.

That all shifted significantly with the 2000 US Census, the first that no longer forced multiracial citizens to choose one racial box. This policy change was the result of years of activism, largely among interracial couples, and often (fascinatingly) led by white mothers of brown children. As a young journalist in the 1990s I distinctly remember coming across one of the magazines published by these advocates and being repulsed by the way it celebrated the "unique" and "special" beauty of biracial children with reverential awe. It was a movement that was not for me, I quickly decided.

Traditional civil rights leaders were also adamantly opposed to efforts to reform the Census and allow a multiracial category. Like me, they remained heavily invested in the power of single-race identity and politics, believing that until we lived in a culture that was no longer systemically and institutionally racist, we were all in this together. By necessity, we had to accept that despite our various gradations and shades, in this society, we were all regarded as one thing: *Black*.

If I were honest, I was also bored by the whole "tragic mulatto" narrative that even I had contributed to as a young woman. I'd first written about being biracial at age twenty-one, roused by a hurtful comment from a professor. She didn't mean anything by it, I'm sure, but her comment had stung anyway. The essay, which I called "Light-Skinned-ded Naps," spilled out of me in a voice that was, in hindsight, more whining than I would have liked. In the years to come, I grew tired of that voice. That story.

But now, as I looked around, I saw that there were mixed-race student clubs and affinity groups on nearly every college campus, along with mixed-race anthologies and essay collections. The experiences and frustrations of being "both and neither" were being widely and openly shared for the first time in our culture. I watched my students navigate these changing times, and as I did, I couldn't help wondering if my own perspective on race had also morphed into something different from what it once had been.

For all my hardened cynicism on the subject, even I caught myself staring at the Black man and white woman in line with their toddler at Au Bon Pain at Miami International Airport and wondering, What had they gone through to get where they were? What did the future hold for them? The questions weren't new, but were they still worth asking? I wondered what had changed, if anything, for them. I wondered what had changed, if anything, for the rest of us. Clearly, the way we were seeing race as a country—or trying not to see it—was shifting for us all.

At that point I'd been with Alfonso, a Spaniard, for about a decade. We were living in a largely Latin city and raising a brown-skinned child of African American and Southeast Asian descent. I did a tally, noting that Haiti, Singapore, Colombia, Canada, Germany, Brazil, Mexico, Spain, Senegal, the Dominic Republic, Lebanon, and Pakistan were each represented in our small circle of friends in Miami, and that only two of them were actually born in America. Brownness was a given in Miami, but not in the way I was used to.

I took these ideas to the *Washington Post* and was given an assignment to write on the topic. Later, I would expand this work, completing a six-part series on multiracial identity for Medium.com (back when they were paying reporters). One of these articles, a piece that described Tacoma, Washington, as a kind of multiracial mecca, did especially well and was picked up by Pocket, garnering more than 187,000 online views and 28,000 complete reads. The numbers confirmed my hunch that this topic had become timely for many readers.

I decided to attend the Mixed Remixed Festival in Los Angeles, an annual gathering for multiracial families, as a start. While there, I was hoping to process some of my own thoughts—to explore how growing up biracial in my day was different from the experience of the multiracial families I now saw around me. That was my intention, anyway. But as it turned out, destiny had something much bigger in mind.

The Los Angeles Theatre Center on Spring Street was packed with mixed-race families and children, many of whom wore trademarked T-shirts that said "I Am a Story." In a standing-room-only workshop, I watched as a facilitator engaged the crowd.

"Why did you come today?" she asked the audience, her "I Am a Story" T-shirt torn at the neck, à la Madonna.

"I'm mixed!" someone shouted from the crowd. "Cambodian and Mexican."

"Love it!" The facilitator fanned across the stage.

"I'm Lithuanian and Black," another offered.

"Love it!"

As I listened to the chorus of voices, it occurred to me that what was happening in the room went beyond race. It was about community and humanity, and about people who had gone through their entire lives feeling alone and isolated. I realized that I had been just like these attendees thirty years ago. I had sat in their same seats. But now, I understood things that I had not been able to articulate as a young person. I saw that there is a time in life when one's sense of self is inherently insecure. There is a time, for everyone, when we're faced with self-doubt. These ordinary human desires and fears are only complicated by multiracial identity.

Now, the passing years had delivered me to another place.

The results of a DNA test proved what I already knew: African roots were only a fraction of my heritage, 36 percent, to be precise. The numbers, while interesting, were irrelevant, at least to me. There would always be those who would not understand why I chose my blackness. But that no longer mattered. I was no longer the confused biracial college student that I had once been. I knew exactly who I was and who I was not.

Just as I was processing these thoughts—lo and behold, the synchronicity—I spotted Jaime, my college boyfriend, ordering a glass of red wine during the evening cocktail reception. As he turned to face me, I saw a slightly weathered version of his younger self. If my father was the first man I had loved unconditionally, Jaime had been the second.

"I don't believe it!" he exclaimed.

We embraced, and he introduced me to his wife and two sons.

"You have a beautiful family." I nodded at both parents. "You must be very proud." I showed them a picture of Olivia and Alfonso and asked Jaime about his parents, whom I had adored. We updated each other briefly before saying our goodbyes and wishing each other well. Still, there was more that I had wanted to say. *You were good to me all those years ago. I'm sorry for the pain I caused you.* Perhaps Jaime's forgiveness had been there all along. Or perhaps I'd never allowed myself to digest it until that very moment. But I felt it there, in that room. It was large and warm and strong. I thought about it for a long time after my return to Miami.

"Zook is Dutch," I explained to a few friends. "Actually, it's Amish."

"Oh, is your father Amish?" one of them asked.

I smiled. My father. Now, there was a name I hadn't uttered in years.

"No. Actually, he's the extreme opposite. My father was wild. A bohemian adventurer . . . and, I guess, a drugged-out hippie strung out on heroin and booze. He was hanging out on Venice Beach in the 1960s when he met my mother." I told my friends about how I'd pulled off the highway in Camarillo, California, and found my half brother. And about how my father came to my graduation ceremony to see me receive my doctorate, crying from his seat as he watched me walk across the stage. As I spoke of him, I realized that the old angst was gone. Now, my father felt like an impartial fact. Kind of like the weather. Sometimes sun, sometimes rain.

Back in Miami, after the conference, these thoughts led to more thoughts.

If Jaime could forgive me, I wondered, could I find a way to forgive those who had harmed me as a child? My father once said to me that forgiveness is contagious. "Invite your heart to come out of the rain," he wrote in one of his meandering poems. Now, a crazy idea danced through my imagination. What if I could forgive him, too? Just let it go? I didn't have anything to lose, I decided. I was already fatherless. Risking my heart again couldn't make me any *less* fatherless. And what if it worked? If it worked, well, that would be something.

Olivia could have a grandpa.

23

forgiving

It was a Saturday afternoon in July when I called my father's home in Vashon. If he answered, it would be the first time we'd spoken in fourteen years. The truth was, I didn't even know if he was alive. I'd found what seemed like a recent photo of him on my younger brother's Facebook page and thought it was worth a try.

My father answered on the first ring. "Well, hello there!" His tone was exuberant. "It's about time we talked! I'm really, really excited to hear from you." We made small talk for a moment and then he paused. "Kristal, I owe you a huge apology. My head wasn't in the right place back then." He told me that not long after Michele's death, he, too, was diagnosed with bladder cancer, the same disease that she had. He underwent two surgeries, beating the disease back, but, on the heels of that, also underwent heart surgery. Something went wrong during the operation, which ended up lasting nine hours. The road to recovery had been long, he said.

"I'm so sorry to hear that. . . . It sounds awful. But I'm glad you're healthy now." I'd never been one to mince words. Now, sleep deprivation and menopause made me even less likely to do so. "I was in a very different place too, back then. I was confused and full of questions that it seemed like you didn't want to answer. I guess I just got frustrated."

"Huh," my father said simply. I later learned that it was one of his favorite words. *Huh.* He told me that he often used it when sponsoring alcoholics and drug addicts in his twelve-steps program. It means that you accept and digest the information someone is giving you without judgment or defensiveness.

I told him that I was married now, with a nine-month-old daughter, and that I wanted to be in touch again and to know that he was OK.

"Yeah. When you told me you wanted a father and not a friend, that pretty much knocked me off my high horse." His voice softened. "I think about you all the time, though."

"You do?"

"Yeah. I had a girlfriend after Michele died. We were together for eight years. She was a psychologist. Sometimes I'd ask her for advice about you. I'd say, 'Should I call her? Should I try to make up with her? I don't know what I did wrong.' I'd look you up on the internet to see what you were doing and what articles you were writing, but then I'd get sad, so I didn't do it anymore. I took down a box of your letters too, the other day. I was just looking through them on Friday."

"What a coincidence. That's crazy."

"It is."

My father surprised me then, by circling back to my earlier comment—the one about my unanswered questions. "Well, I'll tell you whatever you want to know, sweetheart. I mean it. I'm happy to do that. Whatever I can remember."

I had waited so long to hear those words, said in just that way. There was an openness to his voice now, a certain rawness that I supposed had come with age and suffering. My father was eighty now, with more than forty years of sobriety. He had abandoned not only me but three children before me, a fact that he had carried with him every day of his long life. He had also buried a wife, enduring the kind of loss that must have split him open. No one comes back from that the same as they were before.

We talked for two hours that day, and my father stayed true to his word. For the first time, he stood with me and faced my questions. To the best of his ability, he answered them, one by one.

Earl Zook, my grandfather, was a fascinating character, as it turned out. His official title was business manager, but in essence he was a fixer for MCA studio executive Lew Wasserman. Need a dozen Rolls-Royces? Earl had them priced and delivered. Done.

It was a small world, as I wrote in an email to a colleague when I first learned about my grandfather. Katrina vanden Heuvel was publisher of *The Nation* magazine, whose imprint had published two of my books. She also happened to be the granddaughter of Jules Stein, cofounder of MCA. "Looks like my grandfather worked for your grandfather," I noted, attaching a biographical link from the internet.

A heavy drinker and, later, a pill popper, Earl Zook spent the first eight years of my father's life shacked up in a Hollywood love nest with his secretary, Betty. At eight, when his parents divorced, my father went to live with Earl and Betty and began drinking from their wine bottles. By the time he was eleven, he was a falling-down drunk.

I always knew that he'd been an alcoholic and drug addict. That had never been a secret. What I didn't know was the depths of his despair as a child. I didn't know that his mother, Jean, was a practicing Catholic who never wanted children but did not believe in abortion. Finding herself pregnant at thirty-five, she later made it clear to my father that Earl had raped her. In the hospital, she refused to care for her newborn child or to give Phil any kind of attention, even when he nearly died of an asthma attack at two weeks of age.

When he was growing up, my father's parents often sent him traipsing across town alone, on buses and trains, with a small suitcase, shuttled between an aunt in Sierra Madre and his father and stepmother in the San Fernando Valley. When there was nowhere else to go, Earl, who had worked for Harry and Jack Warner for twenty-five years, told his son to use his lifetime Warner Bros. free movie pass and go sit in a theater for a while.

At twelve, not surprisingly, my father stole a car and ran away. Later, he hitchhiked and hopped freight trains up and down the California coast, drugged and drunk. When a judge sentenced him to Los Angeles County's Youth Authority Forestry Camp for juvenile delinquents, he bonded with the hard-living Chicanos—the *vatos locos*, as he called them—who drank, smoked, and grew marijuana right there on government grounds. To fit in, Phil threw punches and tattooed his inner wrist with raindrops. An initial six-month sentence turned into two years.

By the age of thirty-six, my father had crashed sixteen cars and been pronounced dead twice. A judge sentenced him to an indefinite term at Atascadero State Hospital for the criminally insane, where he was repeatedly given as much as 120 volts of electroshock treatment. "I was shocked and shocked and shocked," he said, "until I was drooling and catatonic." Authorities told him he would never be released from Atascadero. Had things gone differently, he might still be there today.

memories

"How did you and my mother meet?" I asked my father the next time we spoke. We were settling into our conversations now, going back in time together regularly.

"I was living with a friend . . . what was his name?"—he racked his brain for a moment—"Rudy! That was it. Your mom called him 'Nifty Rudy.'" He laughed. "I can't believe I remembered that. Rudy was a dope dealer. *Rudolfo*. Mexican guy. I was staying with him in a motel by the Santa Monica Pier. Your mother knocked on the door one day and I answered." He exhaled for emphasis.

"She's standing there. Oh. My. God. That was it! My heart just flipped." I smiled into the phone. "So, what happened?"

"We took off in my Jag—your mom and me and Nifty Rudy. Went to a nice place way up the coast, a restaurant in Malibu." In those days, my father was driving a 1954 XK140 Jaguar with a walnut dashboard and plush leather seats. He'd conned the dealership by claiming to be Earl Zook, who worked for Lew Wasserman at MCA. The dealer called MCA and confirmed that, yes, an Earl Zook did work there, and after handing over a ten-dollar deposit, my father drove the car off the lot.

At nineteen, my poor mother didn't have a clue about what she was getting into when she met Phil. From her point of view, he had been a respectable bank manager. She had no idea that he'd shot up heroin while working that job. Or that he had smuggled pot from Tijuana, committed fraud, stolen identities and cash, and driven under the influence more times than he could count. Did she know that he had left a wife and three children behind somewhere in the San Fernando Valley? I wasn't sure. These were things my mother didn't discuss in those days. I can only imagine that she admired my father's worldliness—perhaps seeing him as an ex-marine, motorcycle-riding, daredevil adventurer.

Not long after they met, my father used a stolen credit card to charge a stack of suitcases at J. C. Penney. He and my mom announced to Dra that they were leaving town. They lived in Baja California for a while, then in Las Vegas. Later, they rented an apartment in Phoenix. I was stunned to learn these details. My mother had always given the impression that she and my father had an affair, not a common-law marriage. I didn't know that they had lived together at all, much less in several cities.

Their plans unraveled, though, when Mom discovered that she was pregnant. It had happened quickly, in Tijuana. Being young and naive, it took Mom a while to put the pieces together. When she realized what was happening, she told my father she wanted to go home.

"We were supposed to go to New Orleans next, so I could work the oil rigs," my father explained, "but she said no. So I dropped her off at your grandma's house and took off. I did 120 miles an hour through Texas with weed, heroin, and booze in the car."

"Why?" I asked. It was a rather fruitless question to put to an addict, but I wanted to understand him.

"I don't know. Running away."

Six months later, my father was back in Los Angeles. He immediately went to a piano bar and called Mom from a pay phone. They tried to make it work once again. My father worked two jobs, he said, one at a gas station and one delivering vegetables. I could hear the pride in his voice as he ticked them off. "I even bought a car," he added. "I was doing good."

"So, what happened?"

He sighed. "I ran away again. I was always afraid. And I always ran."

The silence between us was honest, with nothing hidden in the empty spaces.

"I didn't see your mother again until after you were born, and then . . . I don't know, Kristal. I just couldn't sit still. I kept running away." I waited for more, but his train of thought seemed to end there.

"Now, listen. I want to say something to you," my father said, shifting the conversation.

"OK."

"I love you."

My eyes stung. There was nowhere for me to go. No defense and no walls. When I answered, I could hear my voice drift out of my body like a faraway feather. "I love you, too. Always have."

"I know, sweetheart. I know."

25

vashon island

I arrived on Vashon Island on a bright afternoon in October 2017, just before my daughter's first birthday. My father and I had been in touch often that summer and fall. We spoke regularly by phone and by text messages that he punctuated with ladybug, butterfly, squirrel, and sunflower emojis. And hearts, too. All kinds of hearts.

I'd visited Vashon before, in my twenties, but something had been missing then. I hoped this time would be different. It was just us now. We would have the space and time to smooth over whatever hard edges remained between us. I knew that soon memories would be all I would have left. This time, I wanted them to be good ones. I wanted to finally have a father, as belated as that might be. This time, I wanted to be able to call him *Dad* and mean it.

My father was gray and bearded when I spotted him at the ferry. He wore his usual uniform: Levis, hiking boots, and a Pendleton flannel shirt, like the *vatos locos*, as he liked to call them, the rebellious youth he came to know while he was locked up in a juvenile detention camp. We leaned into one another for a hug. Afterward, I nodded at his silver ponytail.

"Your hair is long."

"I haven't had a haircut in fourteen years. I'll cut it when our soldiers are out of Iraq and back home."

"Ah."

Still upright and sturdy at eighty years old, he commandeered my suitcase easily, steering it back to his Lincoln Town Car.

"Do you remember Vashon?" he asked as we passed quaint cafés and antique shops.

"Not really." My visits to the island were more than twenty years earlier. An emotional other-life.

"What about this car? Do you remember riding in it?" My father was exceedingly proud of his old Town Car.

"No." I smiled. "Sorry."

He parked near the Hardware Store Restaurant, which doubled as an exhibit room for local artists. Again, he tried to jog my memory, amazed that it could be worse than his. I was amazed too.

"Do you remember when we went to Seattle, to that Mexican restaurant?"

"No."

"Well." He shook his head. "It was a really windy day and you were cold. We couldn't find the place. You got really, really mad."

We found seats inside and I glanced around, looking for a server. It had been a long flight and I wasn't good company on an empty stomach.

"We walked a lot," my father continued. "You weren't too happy about that either."

I shrugged. "Those earlier visits are kind of a blank to me. I don't remember much of anything."

"You mostly stayed in my office." My father stretched his neck forward to emphasize his point. I could see that something about those visits nagged at him. "You asked if you could use my computer and you stayed in there, working."

"That sounds like me. I probably had a deadline."

There was one clear memory I did have, if I was being honest, but I hesitated to share it with him now. Instead, we ordered our burgers, with mushrooms and fries. I sipped my water as we waited, squeezing fresh lemon slices into the glass. Only after we'd finished eating—with a full belly and a clearer head—did I decide to jump back in. It was amazing how food could change my mood. I felt nurtured, whole, ready.

"I do remember one morning." I glanced at him, measuring his reaction. "I was sitting at the kitchen table with Michele, drinking coffee. You had gone to work. She and I were alone together for the first time. I remember seeing her prescription medication on the table. That was when her behavior started to make sense to me. Was it Prozac that she took?"

"No." His tone was defensive at first, but quickly softened. "Maybe Zoloft or Paxil."

"Well. I remember that I was uncomfortable with her. And with Jennifer, too." My father's youngest daughter was in her forties now, a librarian in Seattle with a husband and two children of her own. My father thought about this for a moment, and what he said next stunned me.

"Jennifer was always jealous of you. She felt threatened by you. They both did. Her and Michele."

It was a monumental confession. Words that I never expected to hear him say. They confirmed my deepest suspicions. *I was not crazy.* On the surface, his family had welcomed me, but that was a lie. It felt good to hear him say the words aloud.

My father would not have added race to the equation, but as I turned the events over in my mind, I couldn't help doing just that. I was the unwanted illegitimate daughter of an African American woman, after all. The black sheep of the family, in more ways than one.

"Do you remember meeting your grandmother?" he asked then, as if reading my mind with his own train of thought. At first, the question made no sense to me. For me, there was only one grandmother. *Meeting Dra? I've known her all my life.* But he meant Jean, *his* mother, who came to Vashon to live later in life and who would eventually die there.

"Oh. Not really."

"She was awful." His face fell. "She was so rude. I couldn't believe it."

"To me or you?"

"To both of us."

"Why?"

He shrugged, but there was no way I was going to leave it at that.

"Was it because my mom is Black? And you have a Black daughter?"

"Maybe."

"Did you ever ask her about it?"

He shook his head as though the idea had never occurred to him.

A local stopped by our table to thank my father for being his twelve-steps sponsor. That happened a lot on the island, as I would soon discover. There were all kinds of drug addicts and alcoholics across the Puget Sound who felt that they owed him a great debt. "Your dad is like this national treasure that no one knows about," as one of them would later explain to me. "People don't realize that there's this old man out here who, for us, is like a messiah." Not only had my father been sober for decades; he'd also helped to found and launch the very first twelve-steps program on the island.

I pressed my lips together after the friend left, trying to decide what to make of my father's non-answer. Was my grandmother Jean racist? I wondered. In many respects, my father was the perfect embodiment of a 1960s hippie liberal, the kind who didn't believe he needed to talk about race because he already thought of himself as utterly and inherently without prejudice. In fact, I don't remember us ever really discussing racism, in his family or elsewhere. Although I do remember that once, when I was in my thirties, he referred to himself as "color-blind." "That's not a word you should use anymore," I told him then. "There's no such thing. No one is color-blind. Not even children. It's been proven."

I scratched my head, annoyed. His mother lived to be ninety-four, and in all that time, he never thought to have a conversation with her about her absent biracial granddaughter? As we lingered over our plates, I realized there was something else that I needed to say. I hadn't planned the words exactly. It was more of an instinct, a feeling that things needed to be laid out in the open, like ground rules. I wanted to put them in place now, at the start of our new journey, so that we could get on with the business of being happy together.

I took a sip of my water, aiming for a tone that was factual rather than accusatory, and looked him dead in the eye. "You know, there's still a part of me that will always be that hurt little girl. I mean . . . I don't think we can simply ignore it, or wish it away. That little girl will always want what she wanted and couldn't have. There *is* a sadness in that, you know?"

I thought I saw him flinch. And after everything that he had done and not done, I just couldn't stand to see my senior citizen father suffer in that way. "Don't worry," I rushed in. "That part of me is much smaller than it was before." I smiled. The rope I was trying to walk was treacherously thin. For as much tenderness as I felt toward him, I also knew that the words had to be spoken if our relationship was to be genuine. "But I think we all have that child in us, don't we?" I waited for a response but got nothing. "That little person who just wants to be seen and heard?"

He nodded. "I guess so."

He paid the bill and we settled back into the Town Car.

"Do you feel better?" he asked before starting the engine.

"Better?"

"Now that you got that off your chest."

"I didn't feel bad before."

"OK. Good."

We rode in silence, crossing the portage that led to Maury Island, where my father had relocated some years ago. Maury was even more isolated than Vashon. It had no grocery store, no gas station, no post office, no library. In 1918, when the isthmus connecting the islands was built, there had still been a salmon cannery and shipbuilding yards, but those were gone now, leaving only acres of wildlife and sprawling plots of open land.

My father's home was a modest, fabricated structure laid down on what felt like a vast private forest. Behind the house, there were a woodsy footpath and a perimeter of cherry and crabapple trees. We entered through a side door, secluded by ten-foot-high blackberry bushes. "That used to be full of wildflowers." He gestured at the front porch, now covered with weeds.

"What happened?"

He shrugged. "I guess I figured, what's the point? That's what I did for a living. Now I'm just an old man living alone." How sad, I thought. A toppled bird feeder sat empty, the birdbath next to it full of dried leaves.

"You stopped feeding the birds too?

"Bird feeder was twenty dollars a week. I stopped when Michele died. It was too expensive."

He settled me into a guest room off the laundry that had once belonged to Dominic, his youngest son. There was a slightly broken-down desk for homework and a few pieces of artwork from local plays Dominic had performed in as a teenager.

"Wanna take a walk?" My father walked five miles a day, tracking his steps on an iPhone.

"I'd love to."

Dockton Forest was just steps from my father's front door—193 acres of natural parkland and saltwater shores with miles of footpaths, a massive 470 acres in all, according to the King County website. My father pointed out the names of trees and flowers along the way. "That's a big-leaf maple." The late-afternoon sun filtered through, transforming its leaves into a translucent yellow-green color.

"Maple?"

"Yeah, but not the kind that makes syrup."

I picked up a cone.

"Conifer. From the fir tree."

There was a loud clicking sound. "That's a woodpecker." He pointed to a tiny creature, ticking away. I'd never seen one up close. It was so much smaller than I'd imagined. There was something about being there, deep in the natural world, that facilitated our reunion. It was as though the trees listened to what we had to say, too, from a place of stillness and nonjudgment.

"Don't touch those," he warned when we passed nettle bushes. "They'll make you itch."

Here was something I knew about. "Nettle is a liver cleanser," I chimed in.

"That's right. How did you know?"

"I've tried the herbal tea."

He nodded. "My doctor says I only have 44 percent capacity of my liver left." He must have felt something in me clench. "It's OK, though," he added. "I'm not going anywhere." He smiled into my eyes. "I think I can still make it to 105."

That night, we grilled steak on the barbecue and slathered baked potatoes with butter and sour cream. Over the next few days, we enjoyed our unhurried meals together, talking and talking some more. No matter how uncomfortable the conversation got, we kept eating and we kept talking. I discovered that my father relished long, slow meals as much as I did. Maybe it was because his stepmother, Betty, never gave him enough to eat as a child. Instead, he told me that she and Earl would mostly smoke cigarettes and drink booze at mealtime. Betty might make a single egg for my father, with a piece of melba toast, and call it a day. Later that night, I noticed that although we had shared a large fillet of steak—which wasn't much at all, in my book—my father didn't finish his portion. He wrapped the remaining two or three bites in Saran Wrap, as though savoring the thought of having more to eat the next day.

I was beginning to get a better sense of how he had become such a lost little soul as a child. Olivia was not yet a year old, and already I prided myself on cooking nutritious dinners for her and sitting down to eat together. Those moments were sacrosanct. I tried to imagine what scars I might leave on my own daughter if I were to treat her the way Betty and Earl had treated my father.

He pushed his plate aside, indicating that there was more.

"Betty was a mean drunk. I'd come home from school and she'd be lying on the floor with blood all over her. I'd have to call my dad to come take care of her. She told me from the beginning, 'Don't you dare call me *Mother*. I'm not your mother. Call me Betty.'" His eyes clouded over. "I wanted to call somebody *Mother* so badly." He told me that after she died, many years later, he sat by her bedside and talked to her lifeless body for two hours. "She did the best she could," he concluded.

We leaned back in our chairs, listening to the rustling trees. My father and I were both walking the same road, I realized then. We were, both of us, learning how to forgive.

That night, I slept more soundly than I had in months, buried under a pile of blankets and lulled by the brisk night air. At daybreak, I awoke to a full moon and the sight of Dominic's astrological chart of the planets pinned across the ceiling. After dressing, I padded to the kitchen for coffee, catching a glimpse of a deer scampering across the front yard. My father had placed a picture of Olivia on the kitchen windowsill—a favorite of mine. She was in her high chair with Greek yogurt covering her cheeks and fingers and a huge, laughing smile.

I grinned at this, reaching into the cupboard for a coffee mug. But what I found there made my heart skip a beat. Turning the mug, I read the inscription: *Just when the caterpillar thought the world was over, it became a butterfly.* How fitting, I thought, remembering the sermon that Jaime had once shared with me. My father and I had transformed. Now, a new way of life awaited us both.

thanksgiving

Mom was "thrilled" that my father and I had reconnected, she wrote to me in an email. "Reconciliation is always a good thing." If her feelings went deeper than that, she didn't say. Mom had worked her way up the career ladder over the years from secretarial positions to working for judges as a judicial aide, reading and editing their rulings.

Now she lived in a gated senior community in Riverside County, and with plenty of free time on her hands, she was determined to make the most of her retirement years. She socialized regularly at the clubhouse and played in Mexican train and mah-jongg tournaments that went on for hours. She cruised the Caribbean and danced in elaborate, costumed musicals. Busy and active at seventy-three, my mother gave the impression of someone removed from her past wounds. After so many years of struggle, she finally seemed happy.

"It's my mom." I passed the phone to my father after breakfast one morning. "She wants to say hello." I suppose I could have given them their privacy, but there was no way I was going to miss their first conversation in a quarter of a century.

My father didn't seem to mind. Every now and then, he glanced at me with a smile or a nod as they chatted. Then, after a while, I thought I heard something shift in his tone. Wait a minute. Was my father actually *flirting* with my mother? I watched, stunned, as he jotted down her email address and promised to send a picture.

After he hung up, I stared at him long and hard. "Wait. What just happened? Did you ask her for a picture?"

"Yeah, and she asked for mine."

A question had been lingering in the back of my mind for more than two decades. Now seemed like as good a time as any to ask it. I studied him closely. "Is it true what you told me before, at my graduation in Santa Cruz? That she was the love of your life?"

He didn't hesitate. "I still love her."

"What do you mean?"

He crooked his neck slightly. "Your mother and I weren't together very long . . . but that was the feeling I had. That I still have. I don't know. It's a little hole somewhere. When I think of her, my heart still does a little 'thump, thump.'" He paused. "It would be nice to be friends."

My parents talked every day after that, sometimes two or three times a day. They shared the same memories, liked the same music, got the same jokes. When I broached the subject of my father with her, Mom's voice became uncharacteristically dreamy.

"Is he the same as you remembered him?"

"Oh, yes. He was always sweet. And he's still the same." She called him poetic, reading an email he had sent. "It says my spirit has allowed the embers of love to be rekindled, and that the fire is burning bright."

"So, he is flirting with you."

"Yes." I could hear her smile over the phone. Then, to my astonishment, my reticent mother added, "It's like we're falling in love all over again."

My father was certainly speaking the language of romance to Mom. He had volumes of original poems, and from time to time he dug one up and sent it to us both:

These old once calloused hands that could pull a blackberry bush
    without gloves are attached to arms that are still alive and be-
    coming soft piano/poetry tools

The hearing is bad and the eyesight, glassed, but the voice and
heart are still strong

and loved by some.

Mom heard his words not as a senior citizen but as the girl that she
once was. The one who had trusted him.

"Are you still being reserved?" I asked her one day.

"Oh, no!" She laughed. "Not anymore. He's taking me back to a time
when I really did believe in a bigger kind of love. I feel safe now, going
back to that place."

If that was true, I thought, then my father really had accomplished
something remarkable indeed. Something that perhaps no one else had
ever done, or ever could do, in all the years of my mother's life. He had allowed her to be vulnerable again. It was a sea change that would soon transform everything about my mother, including her relationship with me.

I asked Mom if it would be OK with her if I invited my father for Thanksgiving dinner at her house that year, and she agreed.

From that point on, my fantasies ran amok with possibilities as I day-
dreamed about my parents' impending reunion. I thought about them as
I jogged by the marina, where there were boats with names such as *Seas
the Day*, *Sunday Morning*, and *Diamond Ring*. Maybe they could live on
a boat, I thought. Or, what about in Mexico? My father once wrote to me,
long ago, that he wanted to retire there. In a flash, I was riffling through
old letters, pulling up one he'd written decades earlier in broken Spanish:

Un dia me iré a México para vivir. Cuando tengo muchos años y no
es posible trabajar y no tengo dinero, yo voy.

*One day, when I can no longer work, and when I have no more money,
I'll retire in México*. I even entertained fantasies of all of us traveling
together—maybe even flying to Spain to spend Christmas with Alfonso's
family.

But just as quickly, I canceled out these fantastical musings. After all,
Mom was all about French-tip fingernails and champagne cruises, while
my father preferred blue jeans and hiking boots and certainly would not

be found anywhere near a bar. There were huge lifestyle differences between them. He lived in a wild forest. She, in a neatly manicured gated community. She watched television for hours on end, with a haphazard sleep schedule. He preferred to play the piano on a Sunday morning, rather than binge in front of a screen. Moreover, he liked living alone, as my father reiterated repeatedly.

I worried that Mom would get her hopes up and have her heart broken again . . . along with mine.

A few days before his arrival, my father told me that he had something he wanted to say.

"OK." I waited.

"You know that I'm enjoying talking to your mother and getting to know her again."

"Yes."

"But I want you to know, that's not what this trip is about. It's about you, Kristal. And Alfonso. And Olivia. I'm going to Los Angeles to be with *you* and with *them* and I want you to know that. Is that OK?" It sounded more than OK to me. The little girl in me sang out with joy. My daddy was coming to see *me*, woo-hoo!

"We just landed." My father breathed a sigh of relief into his cell phone. The short trip from Seattle, Washington, to Burbank, California, had been treacherous. The night before, he had taken a bus to the Vashon Island ferry, followed by another bus and then a train. From there, he checked into an airport motel to be sure he would be on time for his 7 a.m. flight. He insisted on doing it this way no matter how many times I suggested using Lyft or Uber. In fact, he'd even "practiced" the entire journey two weeks earlier, with a friend, tracing his steps by bus, ferry, and train to prepare. Yet, for all his careful planning, nerves and stress had taken a toll.

My father had managed to sleep for only an hour or so at the motel before setting out for the airport, on foot, at 3:30 a.m. I'd told him that there were airport shuttles, but he wanted to do it his way, and he had arrived at the airport sweating and dehydrated. To make matters worse, it was too early. The airport was closed. Which meant that he had to walk back to the motel and repeat the same trip an hour later.

There was more. While passing through security, he'd lost his eyeglasses and, from that point on, had been unable to make out gate numbers or my text messages. A pang of guilt shot through me. Was I wrong to have asked an eighty-year-old man to make such a trip alone?

"I can't wait to see you," he said into the phone. "And to meet Alfonso and Olivia."

"Me too. We're right here at baggage claim, waiting for you."

A wave of relief washed across my father's face when he saw us. "I made it!"

When we embraced, he felt thinner than I'd remembered him being just a few months earlier. Alfonso clapped him warmly across the back. "It's so good to meet you, finally!" They laughed together, relieved. Then my father gazed down at Olivia, and I watched his features soften and melt. I had dressed her in a poufy blouse with red hearts for the occasion, along with leftover Fourth of July stars-and-stripes sneakers. Instantly, he teared up at the sight of her, causing my own eyes to moisten as Alfonso snapped photos of the three of us—father, daughter, and granddaughter—together for the first time.

"Can I hold her?" he asked.

"Of course." I passed Olivia into his arms.

"Oh!" Tears rolled steadily down his cheeks. "This is what I've been dreaming about."

Afterward, we piled into a rental car, heading for Mom's house in the desert.

"She likes you," I told my father, who sat next to Olivia in the back seat of the car, playing.

"I was always good with kids, believe it or not."

When his first son, Michael, was born, my father was taking night classes at Pasadena City College on the GI Bill and working as a milkman for Adohr Farms. Now, he told me stories that I'd never known about his early days as a new father. "I'd come home from class and sit up with him," he said, "rocking him to sleep until it was time for me to go to work at 3 a.m." In my mind, my father had always been a drunk and a drug addict. I'd never pictured him rocking a baby to sleep. Of course, he was on speed the whole time, he added, using it as a substitute for sleep.

So, there was that.

Had he changed, or had I? I wondered as I watched him talking and joking with Olivia. If there had been a generational curse against us, as my grandmother once believed, then was it also possible that there could be generational blessings? Despite his long absence and his many mistakes, was my father finally becoming my dad? The journey to get here had been torturous, but now, I began to believe for the first time that our family might truly heal.

lisa

"Zoo-kie!" Mom sang out as she opened the front door, giving me a big hug. Lisa rushed over behind her, and we made funny faces and spoke in silly voices, as we always did. Dra shuffled over from the couch, too, overwhelmed, and happy to see everyone together. Although she had adored Phil in the old days, I wasn't sure if she even knew who he was at this point in her disease. Dra never let on either way. She simply hugged and accepted my father just like any other member of the family.

My uncle Arthur was there, too, offering up goofy bear hugs and cracking his usual jokes. Although he'd been largely absent during our childhoods, his life had also taken a turn over the years. He'd showed up regularly to family events for the past two decades or so, when we played dominoes and Mexican train and gorged on dinner and desserts. What's more, he and his wife, Kitty, had both been there in San Jose, helping to see after me when I was a lonely graduate student at UC Santa Cruz.

As we all laughed and hugged and greeted one another, I paused to take it in, realizing that this was, at least for me, a crucial moment. I studied my parents closely, on the lookout for clues as they embraced. It didn't take long. My mother and father gazed into each other's eyes, and the truth became obvious to everyone in the room. Despite having been apart for fifty years, and despite everything they'd gone through and all the hurt and pain of their past, my parents were well and truly in love.

Again.

When it came time for our family tradition of standing in a circle, holding hands, and offering prayers of gratitude, I stood with my father on one side and Alfonso on the other. "My cup runneth over," I began. "I am so grateful to you, God, for the blessings you have bestowed upon our family."

"Yes, Lord." I heard Dra's affirmation, my eyes closed. Lisa was next, then Mom, and so on. We all had something to be grateful for on this day, and every day of the year. That simple knowing was the reason Thanksgiving had always been my hands-down favorite holiday.

The next morning, Alfonso, my father, Olivia, and I took a walk around the neighborhood. I pushed Olivia in her stroller while my husband and father walked ahead, locked in intimate conversation. To my astonishment, they had become instant buddies, already bestowing nicknames on one another. When they paused to check out a street sign, I watched as my father pointed and made a joke—something about poop or butts— and they both doubled over with laughter.

"Give me those bags. I can carry that." Whenever my father saw me struggling with Olivia, he leaped in to help. Over the course of our long weekend together, he rocked my little girl to sleep and read her books; he talked and played with her. He even kept track of what time she ate and went to bed, so that he could be there at the right moment to help out. He was a good grandfather. Better than good, actually. And he remained true to his word that Thanksgiving, staying close by my side during the entire visit. If he and Mom wanted to take a walk, he always asked, genuinely, if I wanted to come along. Not once did he forget the reason he had come to Los Angeles and the promise he had made me.

When our holiday visit came to an end, Lisa and I bawled like children. I wasn't sure why at first, and then a strange thought occurred to me. I now, suddenly, had both parents, while she had neither of hers. There was a sadness in that, and I wondered if we both sensed it, perhaps unconsciously. Whatever she may have felt about the loss of her own mother and father during all those years of our childhood, Lisa kept those emotions to herself. Still, we knew that neither of us would ever have summer campouts with our fathers as girls, or teenage movie nights together. Those possibilities were lost forever.

I longed for the days when Lisa and I had been so closely wedded to one another as children, our destinies interwoven by blood, color, race, and upbringing. Every family has its stories, and there was one that we all loved to tell and retell. We laughed about it, because it showed how, even as a little girl, she had already cultivated a toughness about her and a sharpened way of existing in what must have felt, at times, like a very cruel world indeed.

It happened on a weekday morning, when Mom's beaten-up Corolla was back up and running. She dropped us off at McKinley Elementary School's day-care center in an unusually frantic rush. Lisa and I grabbed our lunch bags and slipped out mere seconds before Mom put the pedal to the metal, making a quick U-turn in the parking lot and hightailing it to work. She must have been distracted that day, wondering if the car would even make it the ten miles to Beverly Hills. Mom was starting a new office job in a dermatology office. She had to be on time.

The empty school parking lot didn't surprise us. We knew it was one of those sort-of holidays when banks were closed but Mom and Dra still had to work. They must have assumed that although our school was closed, the adjacent day-care center would remain open. Lisa knocked on the front door, but there was silence on the other side. We waited a while longer, knocking again and again, until a sinking realization began to take hold between us. I was the first to panic. "There's nobody here!" I cried. "What are we going to do?" Seeing Lisa's confused expression, I added, "I want my Mommy!"

"Shut up, and let me think!" Lisa famously replied.

She was only sixteen months older than I but already behaved like a miniature adult. Even as a child, she was quick on her feet. Street-smart. I watched as she ran various scenarios through her small head.

"But what are we gonna *do*?" I tugged at her sleeve.

She pursed her lips, staring at the heavy traffic along Santa Monica Boulevard. "Should we go to the candy store?" I suggested. Lisa ignored this, wisely. Instead, she took my hand and set out in the opposite direction. In a stroke of genius problem-solving, she had remembered that Saint John's Medical Center was nearby. Mom and Dra often took us there for vaccinations. *Safe people would be there*, she reasoned to herself. *Doctors. Nurses.*

I wonder what they must have thought of us at Saint John's—two little biracial girls looking for their parents. Lisa bravely gave our names at the front desk, explaining that we got our shots there and that we needed them to find our parents. Mustering up our medical records, the staff located the name of an employer, a Mrs. Janet Mendel in the Pacific Palisades, where Dra cleaned house. Once the staff reached Dra, she, in turn, called Mom at the dermatology office, who sped over in the Corolla to retrieve us. Even Lisa's usual cool expression melted at the sight of her aunt. She had been more scared than she let on, of course. But this was also the story of our lives. Brave exteriors belying inner terror.

Only now, as Lisa and I said our goodbyes, did I realize that maybe I'd gotten it wrong all along. Maybe our roles weren't as fixed as I'd once thought. Maybe I had my own brand of strength, tucked just beneath my innocence. And maybe Lisa harbored unspoken vulnerabilities beneath her facade of bravado.

I thought about how proud she'd been as a girl when her father showed up to her Girl Scouts award ceremony. Posing with him for a photo, she looked like she would explode with happiness. And I thought about how she'd once so carefully set the table at her father's apartment, arranging plates just so, for dinner with the woman she hoped would become her new mother. I saw her laying out silverware and cups in my imagination, her face scrunched in concentration, doing her best to be the perfect daughter. As if perfection might have saved her. As if it might have saved any of us.

A thought occurred to me then, just as we were about to load into our respective cars. I whispered it into Lisa's ear, carefully, with a sense of joy and hopefulness. "He can be both of our fathers." I stared into her eyes, wanting desperately to take the pain of her past away. "OK?"

Lisa pulled back ceremoniously, studying me, our expressions those of children making a grave pact.

"OK," she agreed.

rekindled

We had not yet landed home, in Miami, when Mom emailed me a fresh itinerary that she had just purchased from Alaska Air. She announced that she would be spending Christmas and New Year's Eve on Vashon Island, with my father. It was a romantic development that should have left me overjoyed, and part of me was thrilled for them both. If there was a tugging doubt in the corner of my mind, I did my best to ignore it.

In anticipation of Mom's visit, my father hired a housekeeper for a thorough cleaning. I could hear excitement and nervousness in his voice as he told me about his preparations. We were all trying to buy back time. Making up for our losses. He planted wildflowers for the first time since Michele died, he said. There were Shasta daisies, California poppies, purple foxglove, and make-a-wish dandelions. I prayed that the love between my parents would offer them a new beginning and another chance at happiness.

I was leaving my office at Hofstra on a cold January morning, headed for LaGuardia Airport and my commute back to Miami, when my cell phone rang. It was my father, calling to tell me that Mom had gone back to California earlier than expected.

"We had a pretty big brouhaha," he said.

My heart sank. "What happened?"

"I don't know." There was sadness and confusion in his voice. "She found this old purse of Michele's that was in the bedroom closet and . . . I don't know. She got really mad." My mother would later say that she didn't "find" it, but rather that my father showed it to her, simply to needle her. It made no difference who did what, really. What stood between them was obvious: their unresolved past.

The argument had spiraled into treacherous terrain, across minefields of old questions and hurts. One by one, the bombs had exploded. If he loved her so much, why didn't he go back and find her after Michele died? Mom wanted to know. It was a fair question, and one I'd often wondered myself. But my father seemed dumbfounded by her rage, saying that he'd looked for her but there was no listing under her old name. That was true, too. Mom had stopped using her middle name long ago and, after her brief marriage, had taken a different surname than the one my father would have known.

"Well, why didn't you just ask Kristal for my number?" Mom insisted. Another fair point. Although it's also true that my father and I were estranged for many years immediately after Michele died. Perhaps he thought that would complicate things.

"I guess I just decided that if the Universe wanted us together, she would make it happen," my father argued. "And look, she did!" His tone was triumphant, which only enraged my mother more.

"The Universe did not make the decision," she said angrily. "*You* did." And with that, she packed in a huff and went home, regretting her departure the instant she left.

While my father had the benefit of decades of counsel, introspection, and healing through his twelve-steps program and support network, Mom had none of these things. She had survived all these years not by expressing her fears but by doing precisely the opposite, "stuffing them," as my father liked to say. I knew all about the barriers she had erected to protect herself. She'd passed this same strategy on to me. But after everything she had been through, could my father blame her?

We sat in silence for a moment.

"She's afraid," I said.

"I know."

"You left her once before."

"Yes," he acknowledged heavily. "I did."

The brouhaha eventually blew over and my parents once again set about planning Mom's return to Vashon. This time, she would stay for a while, they decided. This time, they would work hard to create a life together.

"I thought you just wanted to be friends?" I asked my father when we spoke next.

"Things change!" His tone was exuberant.

"So, you don't want to live alone anymore?"

"Nope. I changed my mind. Is that OK with you?"

"Sure." I laughed.

"We're cooking mac and cheese," he texted me during Mom's next visit, adding smile emojis, flowers, balloons, and ladybugs. The sun shone brightly on their faces in photographs, as they huddled together in winter coats and hats. In one, Mom's cheek rested on my father's shoulder, the deep maroon of her lipstick matching his scarf so perfectly that it was as though they'd coordinated the colors. I stared at their relaxed expressions for a long time.

"Lovebirds on the stairway to heaven," my father texted.

In another picture, I could almost hear their laughter as they attempted to recover from what appeared to be a real side splitter. Mom's cheeks flushed as she leaned sideways into my father's arms. As he caught her, his smile stretched wide.

"We are revamping, and I am glad with the results," my father wrote. They cleared away old furniture in the house, dusting away memories. "All is well. We are laughing and loving each other."

In July, they joined throngs of visitors at Vashon Island's annual Strawberry Festival, an international affair with a parade and dozens of bands that was attended by literally thousands of tourists. On quieter days, they rode the ferry to Tacoma for reflexology foot massages and shopping at Target. Often, Mom played mah-jongg at the Vashon Public Library while my father attended his twelve-steps meetings. At night, they played cribbage together and watched television. "The weather continues to be perfect here on the Island," Mom wrote in an email. "Our days are passing very pleasantly."

After several peaceful months together, my father decided to sell his house so that he and Mom could move into a two-bedroom condominium closer to town. It was safer, they reasoned, closer to the grocery store and the fire department in case of emergency. I could hardly believe my ears. More than fifty years later, my parents were finally creating a life together.

I remember receiving one photo from that time period that spoke to me more deeply than any I'd ever seen. Usually, my mother maintained her public persona quite carefully, wearing cute reddish-brown wigs with sweeping bangs. It had been years since even I had seen her real hair. But one day, as she cleaned the kitchen on Vashon, my father snapped a candid of her. She was deep in concentration, wearing spandex shorts and a tank top, her natural hair slightly misshapen and kinky. I loved that picture beyond words, in ways that I find hard to explain, even now. In it, I saw the mother that I had so often missed throughout my childhood and adult life. I saw the trueness of her: emotionally present, authentic, and exposed. In that single image, I saw another side of a woman who had kept her innermost person hidden throughout her entire life.

Even from me.

Still, despite their happiness together, my parents couldn't escape the old wounds that threatened to reemerge at every turn. Mom was never good at demur. She challenged what she saw as injustices aggressively and with a sharp tongue. If she and my father disagreed by email, she used all caps and bold as though she were shouting. In their final photographs together, I saw that she was as beautiful as ever, with a hint of midnight blue on her eyelids, but her eyes were brown pools of sadness. In my father I saw only exhaustion and resignation. My heart ached as I watched them flail about.

"Please don't throw away what we have," Mom once said to my father. "We are a match. Getting tripped up over the past doesn't mean we are not a match." She confessed to me, in a wrenching moment, that part of the problem was that she was terrified of being vulnerable. She remained afraid of every kind of emotional intimacy, not only with my father but with me, too. Her honesty stunned me, while also drawing me closer to her in a way that we had never quite managed before.

My parents deadlocked, staying apart for months.

Of course, during this time, my father enjoyed a thriving community of support—an entire town that adored him—as well as a daily spiritual practice to keep him grounded. Mom, on the other hand, suffered through her sadness as she always had. Alone. To my amazement, I learned that Lisa and Dra didn't even know she'd been living on Vashon. Mom told no one, revealing nothing about her relationship with my father to anyone but me.

"Why can't she open up to people?" I complained to Lisa.

"Oh, you know your mom." She sighed. "She's always been . . . elusive. If that's the word."

My mother thought she was protecting herself by staying closed.

She wasn't.

Years later, I would do an interview with Shardé Davis, PhD, an assistant professor of communication at the University of Connecticut, who argued in her book that African American women long ago resolved that we needed masks and walls to survive. "We know that it's destructive," she told me. "We know that it may not be the best way to attend to our mental or physical health. But we have accepted that the benefits of strength behavior outweigh the costs. Strength is functional. And we need to be able to function."

Then came a breakthrough: Mom attended her first twelve-steps meeting. She went back again, with my father's encouragement, until soon, meetings were a regular part of her life.

"Do you think it's making a difference for her?" I was chatting with my father as I pushed Olivia around Coconut Grove in her stroller.

"Oh yes! They're making a *huge* difference. Now we talk. We don't argue anymore. And if it gets to a certain point she says, 'I'm going to have to leave it there for now,' and we hang up."

"Really?"

"Yeah, really!" In fact, he told me that he was planning to come to Los Angeles to stay at Mom's house for a while.

"Oh, that's great!"

"Yeah. We're back!" he added joyfully.

My mother had just picked my father up from the Burbank airport in Los Angeles when Lisa called with terrifying news. Dra had suffered a stroke and fallen on her bathroom floor. I was distraught. How bad was it? Should I fly to California? I was desperately in need of reassurance. But since Mom never bothered to charge her cell phone, or even to turn it on, I had to count on my father for an update.

He answered on the first ring.

"Hi, sweetheart. We just got to the hospital. I'm with Mom and Grandma. Don't worry. She's fine. We're about to see the doctor."

Relief washed over me. It is heart-wrenchingly difficult to explain what this kind of response means in a family where, so often, physical presence doesn't guarantee attention. We weren't people who answered phones on the first ring. You were lucky if we answered at all.

"Everything is OK," my father continued. "We've got Judge Judy on the television in her room. Grandma's alright."

Grateful tears streamed down my cheeks. I was doing that a lot lately—crying. I discovered that, with my father, I never had to buckle up or bear down, as I had so often done with Mom and Dra. Tears flowed openly and often in his presence, and that was OK. He understood emotion and fear, accepting them without judgment or fanfare. Just as Alfonso had shown me so many years earlier, my father confirmed that feeling was part of everyday life. He helped me normalize something that never should have been unusual in the first place.

Dra recovered quickly, thankfully. In fact, her comeback immediately became the stuff of family legend. She was up and about, back to living alone in her own apartment. We even chuckled, gratefully, at how the walker given to her by hospital staff sat unused in a corner of her living room, collecting dust.

rage

I made my way back to Vashon on a sunny afternoon in July 2017. My father met me at the ferry, just as he had done the year before.

"Wow." I pointed to his feet.

"Yeah. They're new." He'd splurged on a pair of brown hiking boots over Christmas for the wedding of his granddaughter, one of two daughters of Eric, his second son.

"I could never wear orange," he added, looking down at my Nikes. They were, in fact, gray, with orange swoops, but no matter.

I smiled. "Why not?"

"They would make me stand out too much. I like to blend in."

We were still getting to know each other in so many ways.

"Do you like tuna melts?" he asked when we stopped in town for groceries.

"Love them."

"OK, good. I'll make some while you're here." He pulled a Post-it from his pocket, adding to a grocery list with hands that I noticed now trembled.

Back home, he put the groceries away while I unpacked and ran a hot towel over my face. I was exhausted, emotionally and physically, and longed for a good night's sleep. Diaper changes plus night sweats and hot flashes made for a lethal combination. I was sleep-deprived beyond recognition. Menopause and new motherhood together in a single, heart-racing package.

I was also frustrated by my mother, who was back in California for the moment. All around our Miami enclave, I saw grandmothers who came to stay with their daughters, sometimes for months, as they adjusted to new motherhood. They organized trips to the park with the kids so that the zombie parents could squeeze in an extra hour or two of sleep. They helped with cooking and shopping. Most importantly, they befriended their grandchildren. Olivia was nearly two now, and my mother had done no such thing.

Just after she was born, in fact, Mom had set off on a cruise to Cabo San Lucas. Other cruises followed, mostly leaving from Miami ports. She was happy to stop by and say hello, but not once had she offered to come and stay, to help me. I was working hard, teaching full time and writing. I'd just finished an *Essence* cover story and had flown to New York for the interview of a lifetime: an in-person sit-down with the legend herself, Oprah Winfrey. (She found the conversation "intriguing," she told her staff afterward, in one of the most meaningful compliments of my career. Smile.)

Still, Alfonso and I both were exhausted. If his parents hadn't been in such poor health, they would have come from Spain in a heartbeat. I couldn't fathom why my own mother showed no similar yearning. Even after all the ways she had disappointed me, I still craved her nurturing, and maybe even some of her homemade beef stroganoff. Her emotional and physical absence began to grate on me in new ways, compounding the hurt I had so often felt as a child. She was hurting me all over again, it seemed. Not only as my mother but as Olivia's grandmother.

I collapsed onto the bed in my half brother Dominic's old room and dreamed heavy, motionless dreams. It was true, I had reunited my family in some ways, and we had come to a new place of understanding together. But in other ways, it was all still a jumble of hurt. I needed to find a way to make sense of my feelings.

Ten hours later, when I awoke, my father and I cooked scrambled eggs with tomato and avocado for breakfast. I thought about the unspoken truth that had haunted our relationship for so many years. When the subject of Michele came up, I seized the opportunity.

"Do you miss her?" I asked.

"I talk to her all the time."

"Oh? What does she say about you and my mom?"

"She's happy about us."

I blinked. "But you said Michele was always jealous of my mom."

"She was. But not anymore. Not after death."

I exhaled. "Can I ask you a difficult question?"

"You can ask me anything you want, sweetheart."

"OK. Well." I steeled myself. "It's just that there's this big, black hole . . . and the question I have is, when you and Michele decided to take care of her sons from her first marriage, and to raise them . . . actually, to have them come live with you . . . what were you thinking about me? I mean, what did you say to each other, about me?"

He considered this for a moment. "That would have been what year?"

I shook my head and tried again to rephrase the question. The year didn't matter. That's not what I was asking. But my father didn't know, he protested. Couldn't remember. I could see that my question was overwhelming him. He was rambling now, trying to figure out addresses, and cities, and states where they might have lived and when. "When you're drinking, you just don't know what you feel," he said finally. "I don't know, Kristal. I'm drawing a blank."

A raging bullet tore through my chest. I struggled to collect my emotions, reaching for a piece of junk mail to use as a fan. My insides were a cannonball of flames. *Anger is just fear*, I told myself. *It won't serve either of us*. I had to redirect him back to the question. I had to force him to look at it squarely and answer. "No, no, no. That's not what I asked." We held each other's gaze. "I'm not asking about when you were drinking."

"OK. What's the question?"

"You were sober." I paused to let this sink in. "I was eight. You wrote me letters. You were trying to make amends. Isn't that what you were supposed to be doing? You were trying to fix your relationship with me."

"I don't remember writing you letters."

"Well, you did. I have two or three of them."

"This was after I got sober?"

"Yes."

"How old were you?"

"Eight."

"What did they say? Were they good?"

"Yes. I loved them."

"And then I stopped?"

"Yes." Our eyes locked. "My question is: what were you thinking about me? What were you feeling?"

We went around and around a few more times, but no matter how I put the question to him, it was clear that my father was simply not going to answer. "I didn't know where you and your mom were," he repeated.

It was my last, most important thing with him. My greatest hurt and open wound. Tears rushed down my cheeks. I was sobbing violently now, my body shaking with rage. "You knew where we were because we called you. I asked my mom to call, and she did. She even had a detective find your address and I wrote to you. I understand that you decided not to stay in contact with me. My question is, *why not?*"

Silence.

"Was it just . . . too complicated?"

"No."

"Were you afraid you'd fail again as a father? Was Michele mad about you being in touch with me? I just want to know *something* about what you were thinking."

My father must have sensed that we could go no further along this path. I deserved the truth. He must have seen that. Because, at that moment, he lifted the veil at long last. "It was probably a combination of all of those things."

The earth came to a halt as I waited for more.

"You're probably right. Michele was probably giving me grief and I didn't want to rock the boat. Maybe that's why we stopped talking that last time, too. I felt that you were disrespecting her memory."

That made sense to me. "Yes. I probably was."

We sat in silence for a moment, an enormous weight falling off my body. I felt light-headed as I watched the leaden burden of our history float out the door and up, into the sky. In yoga, they talk about the sensation between breaths: the space between the inhale and the exhale, where there is no past or future. I felt it then. For the first time in our lives, my father and I existed in the now. I didn't want to hold on to bitterness anymore. Not toward Michele, or him, or anyone.

"Well." I sighed. "She was probably just trying to protect everything that she had built. She felt that all this was hers," I said, gesturing at the house and at him.

He'd told me about how the first five years of their marriage were pure hell, not because my father was drinking but because they had no idea how to get along or to make a relationship work. Michele went to her twelve-steps meetings for family members of alcoholics, and he went to his. Some days, all he did was go to meetings, five or six of them in a row. He worked and went to meetings—that was it. When things got bad, she took a blanket and slept in the car. They persevered.

My father nodded. "I think you probably hit that one on the nail. Michele was jealous of your mother. She was afraid we would get back together. There was pressure and I gave in to it." He met my gaze, nodding, as if to certify his confession.

"Do you want to take a walk?" he asked a moment later.

A walk sounded wonderful. I couldn't think of anything I would rather do.

My mother always said that I had my father's gait. I never understood that. How was it possible to walk like someone you hadn't grown up watching or even seen before? But Mom was right. My father and I were both tall and slim in our blue jeans, and I could see the similarities in our frames as we made our way down the forest's path.

"I feel better already," I said, as we passed a ranch with several long-tailed horses.

"You do?"

"Yeah. Because it's out in the open now and not some big secret. Michele was human and afraid. Just like the rest of us."

Later that evening, my father came to my room.

"I'm gonna miss you." He reached for a hug.

"Me too."

"We got over a big hump this time."

"We did."

My father searched my face. "And now you're pretty complete. Right?"

I nodded, seeing in his eyes how much he wanted me to be.

a birthday

The next day my father's cell phone buzzed with messages and well-wishes. It was his twelve-steps birthday: forty-five years of sobriety. Although he wasn't entirely sure when he took his last drink, he always believed it was sometime around July 1973 and, therefore, decided to call it July 5, the day his youngest daughter, Jennifer, turned one. It wasn't lost on me that she had been the one to give him a reason to stop drinking and not me.

The plan was to celebrate at his noon meeting for alcoholics, and again with the 1 p.m. narcotics group he belonged to as well. He laughed as we pulled into the church parking lot. "I could have joined a twelve-steps program for gamblers too, if I'd wanted to." My father's forearm still bore a faded tattoo image of a pair of dice. He'd gotten it after winning and quickly losing $13,000 in Vegas. "The definition of sobriety is simple," he added. "Clear thinking."

We climbed the stairs to an attic meeting room at the top of the building. There were stacks of books and pamphlets and a small kitchen area with a coffee maker, plates, and utensils. A semicircle of windows provided a view of green trees overhead. As more people entered, someone brought extra chairs out of storage to accommodate the growing crowd. People commented that it had been a long time since that room had been so full.

My father was a gardener by trade, but for the past four decades, sponsoring addicts and alcoholics had been his true calling. When anyone asked him what he did for a living, he always answered with one word. *God.* He tried to live a godly life, he said. If they pressed, he would add, "And I used to mow lawns and pull weeds."

As he introduced me around the room, I was touched to discover that my father had already shared our story with some of the people there. One woman had tears in her eyes as she reached out to touch my arm. "Oh! It's so nice that you could be here!"

"Yes! It is so wonderful that you could come," another echoed. "We've all heard so much about Phil's daughter . . ." Then she added, ". . . the librarian."

The air left the room. At first, no one moved. I shook my head to indicate that, in fact, I wasn't the librarian.

"No?" Her cheeks flushed.

"No," said my father.

"Oh. OK. Sorry."

I felt myself whirling through a rabbit hole. So, it wasn't me that they had heard about after all? It was Jennifer all along? I felt like a fool sitting there, as if I were some kind of special occasion. I had flown six hours from Miami, caught a cab to the Fauntleroy ferry, and crossed the Puget Sound to be with him. I had left my husband and baby girl at home. *What was I doing here?* Time after time, it had been me making the effort to get to know my father. And yet, *I* was the forgotten one?

I sat through the rest of the meeting in a daze. When it was over, a man next to me leaned in, trying to help. "I knew you weren't a librarian." He smiled. Another woman put on a funny voice and struck a comedic pose to make light of the situation. "I don't know nothin' 'bout no librarian!"

I nodded at them both.

"Are you OK?" my father asked afterward.

"No." I bit my lip, feeling like I was five years old all over again. "Did you ever talk about me at all at these meetings?" I peeked at him through my tears.

"Yes! Of course!"

"You did?"

"They know *exactly* who you are."

"OK. Well."

I didn't know what to say to that, so I excused myself to go to the bathroom, a knot of insecurity wrenching in my throat. Try as I might, I could no longer simply reapply my mask of strength. Now that it had been dismantled, it wasn't as easy to reconfigure at the drop of a hat. Maybe this was what Mom and Dra had tried to teach me. Better to simply leave that armor in place, rather than to risk this kind of emotional chaos.

My father waited for me downstairs, outside the bathroom door. He'd packed bananas and water for a snack, which he handed to me now. We ate and drank in the silence of the church, refueling. Afterward, we climbed the stairs again for his second meeting.

The narcotics group was smaller. Those who felt inclined to speak did so. Once finished, they would all end the same way, with the words "That's all I got." For nearly an hour, my father said nothing. It wasn't until the meeting was almost over that he leaned forward, taking the floor. I stared at my hands, afraid of what I might not hear. Instead of commenting on the momentous occasion of celebrating forty-five years of sobriety with his previously estranged daughter, he rambled on about the origins of the narcotics group founded in North Hollywood, even offering up street names where the meetings had first taken place.

For me, it was nothing short of a miracle that we were sitting here together on this momentous occasion, and yet, *this* was what he decided to share? The longer he talked, the more my heart sank. I knew he was proud and happy to have me there, but my father hadn't said a word about it to any of them. Not in this meeting or the one before it. As time inched away, I resigned myself to the reality of the situation. Maybe today simply wasn't as special for him as it was for me.

He paused, wrapping up.

"Anyway . . . my heart is really full. I have my daughter here with me today."

"Yes," one member echoed. There were enthusiastic nods all around. Apparently, I wasn't the only one who'd been waiting for him to address the baby elephant in the room. *Me.*

"Of all my kids, you know, she's the only one who's ever gone with me to any meetings."

"Mmm. That's right." Members sounded off like a Black choir at church.

"Some of you who've been around a long time may have heard me talk about my other daughter and son in past years."

"Yes," the members chorused.

"But those of you who've been coming to meetings more recently have heard a lot about Kristal." He paused. All around, his words were met with nodding agreement. "I'm very grateful for her," he added. I wasn't sure why it had taken so long for him to come to this acknowledgment or why he had meandered in such a roundabout way before making it. But the words were spoken now and I exhaled with relief.

My father bowed his head slightly, adding, "That's all I got."

mothers

My grandmother had made her wishes clear: No artificial respirators. No defibrillator machines. No feeding tubes. The UCLA Medical Center already had the paperwork, she had reminded us repeatedly, carrying an organ donation card tucked safely inside her wallet. She was in her sixties when she first began making these proclamations, not realizing that they wouldn't be needed for another three decades.

At ninety-seven, she suffered her second stroke. This time, she would not recover. Alfonso immediately got on the phone to book a flight for me to Los Angeles. I could hardly see the road through my tears as I drove toward the mountains of Santa Clarita, where only days earlier Dra had been living alone, in good health, in her own apartment. Rushing past the hospital's reception area, I quickly located her room. Lisa was at Dra's bedside, of course, just as she had always been. Ever-faithful Lisa. For all these years, she'd brought Dra cases of soap and soda on the weekends, as did Mom, and kept track of her nurses to make sure they gave Dra her medication at the right times.

I took my grandmother's hand and kissed her cheek. She stared into my eyes, unable to move or speak.

"Is she suffering?" I asked Lisa. "What's happening?"

The medical staff had given her neither food nor water, as was Dra's wish, but now the reality of this plan struck me as unnecessarily cruel. We asked to speak to the doctor again. *Was she dying, literally, of thirst?* A nurse brought something to moisten her lips while several sets of physicians reassured us that Dra was on heavy pain medication and was not suffering in the slightest.

I stepped outside to collect my thoughts. Tapping my cell phone in the sunlight, I scrolled to Mom's name. The information was mostly outdated. She had retired from her courthouse job a decade earlier, but I still had her work number listed. I dialed her cell phone and wasn't the least bit surprised when it went straight to voice mail. To reach her, I had to call my father, on Vashon, who passed her his own cell phone.

"Why aren't you here?" My tone was indignant.

"Oh. I planned to fly back next week when the tickets are less expensive."

I was flummoxed. "Dra may not have a week."

Mom was retired, with a comfortable income. If ever there was time to spend money on a plane ticket, I thought, it was now. For the life of me, I couldn't fathom her coldness. Certainly, her relationship with my grandmother had been fraught. Mom would later describe it as codependent and dysfunctional. But my grandmother had also saved her, a million times and in a million ways. Now, after a life of caring for children and grandchildren, she lay dying, and my mother was a few hours away . . . watching television? It took everything I had to speak the words with a modicum of civility.

Come. Now.

"You're right. It was silly. I'll call the airline."

She arrived without a day to spare. My grandmother left us the next morning, on October 26, 2018, exactly one week after her second stroke. Mom kissed her and caressed her face after she passed—gestures, she later confessed to me, that she could not have easily made while Dra was alive.

My grandmother had lived through many tragedies in her lifetime, but two were always at the forefront of my mind when I thought of her. The first was a mass shooting—a front-page news story that I had grown up hearing about all my life. My family relived it often when they reminisced about Chicago. Apparently, a drug addict who was recently released from prison set out to kill a man named George, who had been flirting with the man's wife. It was true. George flirted with all the women in the neighborhood, including my grandmother, who had taken up with him after her own husband left her and their three small children and moved in with a woman across the street.

The way Dra told it, George at least had the decency to woo her, buying her the first nice dress she'd ever owned and bringing small toys and treats for her three children. Her husband, Arthur Sr., had left her with less than a dollar in change, she said. Dra had gone to the office of the National Urban League and applied for an emergency voucher for thirty-one dollars to get by. In high school I wrote an essay about my family history. I'd never known my grandfather and, strangely, had never even cast him in that light in my mind. Then, as now, I thought of him simply as Dra's husband. But I could see something different in Dra's eyes as she talked about George. He doted on her, she recalled. "He wouldn't even think of coming to my house without a bag of groceries for me and my children."

It was a hot night when tragedy struck. The entire neighborhood sat outside on front stoops, cooling themselves with fans. When the gunman charged onto the street, spraying bullets, he hit George first, who had been sitting beside my grandmother. Dra's stepmother, Big Mama, was seated beside them, and she also went down. Dra raced to the sidewalk to shield my mother, who was just a toddler, and to move her out of the line of fire.

Mr. King, the landlord, whisked victims into the basement, where Dra discovered that my uncle Mervin, then eight, had been shot too—a bullet had blasted through his liver. Once the gunfire stopped, Mr. King piled Dra's family into his new Cadillac, as my mother later recalled, and rushed them to the hospital, where Dra learned that both her mother and son were in critical condition and that George had been killed instantly.

After the shooting, Dra was despondent, broken in a place that would not heal. My mother says she had a nervous breakdown, although there was never any official diagnosis or medical treatment. I do believe that while there would later be other men in her life, Dra would never again be a woman in love. At least, not in that way.

She returned to her day-to-day responsibilities, cleaning houses during the day and working the night shift at a factory job. But the breakup of her marriage and the shooting were only the beginning of her sorrow. Not long after the gunman's rampage, she was walking home from work in the early hours of the morning when a stranger attacked and raped her in an alley. She said nothing about it to anyone. Instead, a violent, inexplicable rash broke out across her body. Stress hives appeared in large, welted clusters, the only visible evidence of her hidden trauma.

Two years after their separation, my grandparents decided to get back together. Perhaps God had cursed them for their mutual infidelities, they thought. Coming together again as a family was a grasp at redemption. It was the kernel that would later become the basis for Dra's paranoia, this idea of a generational family curse. My grandparents reunited, living together, unhappily it seems, for the next twenty years, until my grandfather's death from colon cancer at age forty-six.

Afterward, Dra carried this belief in our family curse with her to California, convinced that her children and grandchildren were destined to grow up without fathers or husbands, convinced that our fate was to struggle alone as women and girls.

I mourned her passing with a heavy, aching sadness. She was a warrior who had defended and upheld her children to the death—even, perhaps, when she should not have done so. I owed so much to her. Dra had made me strong and fearless and determined to claim what was mine. As Lisa later put it, our family was "small, but mighty because of her. Somehow, we were able to overcome, mostly because she taught us to be so fierce as individuals."

I remembered few moments of prolonged physical tenderness from her as a child, but what I did recall was seared into my soul so deeply it sustained me for all the years of my life—like the feeling of her stroking my head as I rested in her lap during the long sermons at Calvary Baptist Church.

Dra taught me to fight. What I did not learn from her, however, was that there was also great power in the heart that knows how to surrender. That part I had to learn for myself.

I had to learn to surrender to outside appearances and judgment, accepting that most people would never fully recognize me in the way that I saw myself on the inside: as a Black woman. I had to surrender to the terrifying possibility of love, allowing my husband access to my vulnerabilities and weaknesses in order for us to share a life together. I had to surrender to the reality that I could not bear children in order to be given the blessing of my beautiful baby girl, Olivia. I had to surrender my anger to forgive my father and allow for a new beginning between us. I had vowed to create the family of my dreams as a child, and in many ways, I had done just that. Through sheer force of will, I had pieced together what was broken, including myself.

But there remained one piece that was not yet mended.

One morning, while I took our dog, Coco, for a walk, I stuck earbuds into my ears, took a deep breath, and dialed my mother's number. It had been weeks since we'd had a real conversation. We chatted about nothing at first, small talk that I found emotionally exhausting. Mom had been attending twelve-steps meetings for some time, at my father's suggestion. She'd even gone to a weekend twelve-steps convention. I had expected to hear about all of this in her usual way. She would tell me about how well things were going by relating basic upbeat facts but withholding any deeper emotions. Coco sniffed at a fire hydrant two houses down and we made our usual turn, rounding the block clockwise. I tugged at him gently, my attention fading. Then Mom said something that stopped me cold in my tracks.

She said she was learning a lot about herself, and about our family, at the meetings. I stopped walking. "There's a woman there with two sons that are both addicted to heroin," she continued, "and it got me thinking about Grandmommy."

We had not talked about Dra since her death.

"I realized that she was really the adult child of an alcoholic," Mom said. "Things she did, and the way she behaved, all the things that I thought were her 'personality,' were actually coping mechanisms."

My gaze drifted toward the blue Miami sky.

Yes.

Six months later, my mother surprised me again, sending an email that would change both of our lives forever. It began with a simple sentence that caused my heart to skip a beat. *This is a letter of amends. Step nine.* Mom said that she had been putting this step off, afraid it would come out wrong, afraid that it wouldn't be good enough. Afraid, afraid, afraid. Until, finally, there was nothing else to do but sink into the abyss and take that leap of faith.

> The purpose of this letter is to acknowledge behavior of mine which has been harmful to you and express my willingness to behave differently in the future.

Immediately, I saw that this was not going to be one of her typical, argumentative emails, the kind that tended toward analysis and a painful kind of wordplay competition, to see who could out-logic the other person. "You're not a lawyer arguing a case," I once complained during one of our disagreements. "Just tell me how you feel."

This was different. The sentences were direct. Straightforward. Subject and verb, just as I taught my journalism students. Who did what to whom? In them, I could hear my mother's authentic, feeling voice, and that was a revelation in itself, and an instant comfort.

> I have said "I'm sorry" many times before and then immediately reverted to the same old behavior. This is not that. This is about me admitting and taking responsibility for harm I have caused you.

She took responsibility for being "emotionally unavailable, distant, cold, critical, uninvolved, passive-aggressive, unsupportive, undemonstrative, argumentative, and resentful." Her list was long and detailed. She acknowledged that she had "failed spectacularly at providing emotional support" at crucial moments in my adult life, like when I had surgery in New York and after the birth of my daughter.

Beginning with this letter, and for many months afterward, my mother began to talk to me and slowly reveal her true, vulnerable self. For the first time, I learned about things she had done that were not flattering to her. She offered them openly, without trying to deflect. It is hard to describe the feeling of deep peace that such words can offer. My mother's amends confirmed that I hadn't imagined or invented my sorrow. Her actions and inactions happened, and they'd left a scar.

I regret not cherishing you during your precious growing up years. . . . I regret the confusing and unsatisfying nature of my conduct toward you as an adult.

The letter went on, addressing every possible lack that I may have felt, then and now, in the hope that her words might help to heal my soul, as she put it. She called me her darling girl and told me that she loved me. I was undone. My mother had come a long way in the name of love. I could feel her yearning through the page. I could feel her loneliness. I could feel her reaching, which is all any of us ever really want and need from those we love.

Someone to reach for them.

Not long after sending this letter, Mom came to Miami for a visit. This time, it would not be a pit stop on her way to an awaiting cruise ship but a real stay, a destination in and of itself. For the first time, she came with the sole purpose of being a mother to me and a grandmother to Olivia. I had never dreamed that I might one day be able to walk my daughter in her stroller, to a grassy park, with my mother by my side. But we did just that. We were chatting about nothing in particular when she casually unloaded a bombshell.

"No one in our family ever hugged each other," she said.

"What?" I was confused. We were a family of huggers. Always had been.

"Not always."

I stared at her. "What do you mean? Dra didn't hug you?"

"Never. Neither of my parents ever showed anyone *any* kind of affection. Not to each other and not to their children. I never once saw my mother and father embrace. *Never.* Not even a kiss on the cheek."

"But Dra always hugged us."

"Not in the beginning," Mom insisted. "Nobody hugged anybody, and we never hugged you or Lisa when you were small."

I shook my head in disbelief. "What changed?"

"Do you remember Tom Mack?"

How could I forget white-haired Tom Mack with the house at the top of Laurel Canyon? Tom Mack with the pool and the sundeck and linguini with clam sauce?

"Yes."

"Well, when Tom came along, it was his habit to hug everybody all the time. So that became our habit too. We learned that from him."

I learned more about my mother in those five minutes than I had in my entire life.

What's more, during that visit, she cared for Olivia with a devotion I could hardly have fathomed just a few months earlier. She read books to my baby and offered to sleep in her room when I had to go out of town for work. I dared myself to lean on her, hoping I wouldn't get my heart dashed against the pavement. Mom came through like she never had before. When Olivia woke up in the middle of the night for a diaper change, my mother was right there. Although she must have been exhausted, I could see on the baby camera in the room that she was nothing short of patient and loving. My mother and daughter began to know one another, creating a bond that would endure.

When Mom returned to California, she knew exactly what kind of gifts to send Olivia in the mail. Something Paw Patrol and something Peppa Pig. The cartoons she knew her granddaughter liked best.

32

transformation

Thanksgiving of 2019 was quiet. Dra was gone, a fact that I still had trouble digesting. Alfonso was also missing that year, for the first time. He had gone to Spain to see his parents, whose long illnesses dragged on. His father, Jose, would pass away not long afterward, leaving Paquita alone in a wheelchair. It was a trying time. I liked to remember my mother- and father-in-law as they'd once been, on the beach at Almería, enjoying their children and grandchildren. After lunch, Paquita always made a habit of racing me to the ice cream shop, getting there first so that she could pay for everyone's dessert before I did.

My heart ached for her, and for my husband.

Lisa planned to join us at Mom's house in a day or two, but until then, it was just the four of us: Olivia, me, and my parents. It took my brain a few seconds to register this as I stared out across the corridor of the Palm Springs Airport and saw them standing together, waving.

Olivia's grandparents.

"Grandma!" Now three, my daughter raced toward baggage claim, flying into my mother's arms. They were buddies now and even enjoyed long, involved FaceTime conversations without me. Just the two of them, talking and sharing news.

As for my parents, the subject of marriage had come up a few weeks earlier, and disagreeing, they had once again decided to go their separate ways. By then, they had broken up and reunited so many times I lost count. But they were friends. That much I could see as I saw them standing side by side.

We piled our luggage into the car, and Mom headed west on Interstate 10, driving slowly in the rain.

"Are you guys hungry? We have egg rolls for a snack before dinner."

"I don't want egg rolls," my father piped up. "But don't worry, I can make myself a peanut butter sandwich."

"Why don't you want egg rolls?"

"They gave me heartburn yesterday."

"Oh, I doubt that."

I couldn't help smiling out the window. They sounded married to me. My father continued to call Mom his "baby doll," offering her gentle caresses at every opportunity. I didn't have a clue what would become of their relationship, but it no longer mattered. Whatever had taken place between them had left its mark. Their renewed bond had the profound effect of opening my mother's heart, allowing her to expose herself to me, with all of her human vulnerabilities. It was like a circle, but where we start isn't always where we end. My quest for wholeness had a ripple effect. Because I had been willing to forgive my father, he had, in turn, helped to heal my mother, which somehow led to healing me in the most profound way possible.

Olivia sang a quiet tune to herself in the back seat of the car. She did that often. I could see that she was truly a happy and balanced little girl. I took her small hand in mine and pressed it against my chest, swallowing a lump in my throat. My dreams had come true. Although not in the way I expected. And not until many decades later, in what felt like another lifetime from the place where I'd started.

"Grandma! Grandma!" Back at the house, that seemed to be Olivia's favorite new word. She sought my mother out at every turn, clamoring for her attention, which Mom gave freely, allowing her squirmy granddaughter to climb onto her body, drape herself around her neck, and hang from her shoulders.

"Want to sit here?" my father offered. "I can read you this book."

"Nope. I want to sit here. By *Grandma*."

"Grandma, where are you?" she called out again on Thanksgiving Day, flitting from room to room in a silver ballerina skirt and sparkly unicorn shirt. "Grandpa, where's Grandma?"

"I think she's in the bathroom."

"Okaaaaay," she sang, trotting off.

After the holidays, we were back home and thrown once again in the mix and chaos of real life, with all the challenges and responsibilities of a brand-new year.

My father answered his phone on the first ring.

"Happy New Year, Dr. Zook!"

"I'm so glad you picked up. A lot is going on. I just wanted to talk."

My father chewed on this for a moment. It was the kind of conversation he liked best, the kind that required some degree of depth and soul-searching. "I don't know, sweetheart. I see your name and I pick up. If I'm in a meeting I keep my phone on vibrate, and if I see it's you, I step outside so I can take it. I know I haven't been a good dad. All I can do now is to try to be here for you today. That's what I try to do every day. I want to be here for you, Kristal. And for Alfonso. And for that precious little girl, Olivia."

I paused to take this in. His impromptu speech was its own kind of amends letter. My father had written and spoken various apologies over the years, although he'd never actually compiled them into a single letter. For example, after learning about my childhood sexual assault, he had sent the following:

I wish I was there to protect you and your mom. I wasn't. I apologize. I love you and I want you to know that I am here now. I am not going to try to justify my wrong behavior. I am sorry. I know that it takes a long time and a lot of work to recover. Thank you for making the effort. I am very proud of you.

"For a long time, I didn't know how to love," he continued now as we chatted. "But you do. Somehow you got that gene." After a while, it was time for his twelve-steps meeting. "I'm going to go inside," he said, "but I'm free again in an hour. We can talk all day and into the night if you want. That's what I'm here for. To try to be your dad now. As much as I can."

Later that day, he texted a photograph with this description: "Dandelions in a pavement crack." My father had gotten in the habit of sending pictures to me on an almost daily basis: ordinary images and extraordinary ones, captured on his iPhone. He sent everything from an antique miniature pink rose to impatiens growing under a deck. And now, dandelions. Weeds disguised as flowers. It was fitting. My phone dinged again. Another photo. But this one had nothing to do with landscapes.

It was an old black-and-white image of me as a toddler. In it, I could see that Mom had plaited my curly hair into two braids, just as she'd always done, meeting her responsibilities and loving me with her whole heart, even in the midst of her own despair. Because the truth was, she had been there. Even when it must have been tempting to leave. She stayed. And she loved me. And she raised me up to be the strong, independent woman that I am today. I had been crying in the picture, clinging to an oversize teddy bear pressed against my chest.

"I have had this one in my office for lots of years," Dad texted.

I tucked my phone away, feeling light-headed. Overjoyed to have such a loving, flawed, and resilient family. Through faith and forgiveness, we had come together at long last. I felt like a young girl again, spinning in circles on the playground in her favorite yellow poncho.